John D. Nugent

NERVES, WORRY AND DEPRESSION: THE WAY OUT

John D. Nugent is a solicitor practising in the midlands. He writes extensively and is now working on his first novel which he ruefully calls 'Boomerang' because it keeps coming back. He lives on the Roscommon shore of Lough Reagh with his wife and three daughters, who share their home with an unruly dog called for Jesse James, a talkative cat named Garfield, a wise rabbit known as Whitney and a goldfish, Jaws.

NERVES, WORRY AND DEPRESSION

THE WAY OUT

John D. Nugent

FOUR COURTS PRESS

This book was set by
Seton Music Graphics Ltd, Bantry
for Four Courts Press Ltd,
Kill Lane, Blackrock, Co. Dublin, Ireland

British Library Cataloguing in Publication Data
Nugent, John
Nerves, worry and depression.
1. Depression. Personal adjustment
I. Title
152.46

ISBN 1–85182–074–4

Printed by
Betaprint Ltd, Dublin

Contents

For Maria and my children
who made the best years better;
and for the brothers and sisters
of life's highway who taught me peace;
but maybe most of all
for the troubled you
with the certain promise
it doesn't have to be that way.

1 Getting to know you

If we are not enjoying life, there is something wrong. If we are miserable, there is something seriously wrong. Life was intended to be a vibrant and joyous thing and if we only know it as a burden to be dragged from day to day, the something wrong is with us. There is, of course, a begrudger's theology that life is a term of trial in a vale of tears, but whether we want to believe that is up to us. Most people are as happy as they make up their minds to be.

If you have picked up this book with more than passing interest it doesn't take much intelligence to guess that you are not enjoying life. If you need to read something about nerves, worry or depression you are probably suffering more than you know. It doesn't have to be that way. Happiness and well-being are the natural human state, our human birthright. It is, however, an unfortunate aspect of living that we can lose this inheritance; and if this happens we must take active steps to regain it. This book will show you how to do that and how your life can be transformed into a wonderful experience. If you are having a bad time, that may seem a heavy claim to make; but just to show you that we play on the same team, let me say something quickly about myself.

For over twenty years I have suffered from depression. At one time the attacks were severe and nightmarish; and so many hospitalisations were required that I often thought a season ticket would have been a prudent investment. Although I

did receive much help from dedicated professionals, it was only when I learned to change certain
attitudes and take to living by certain principles
that a real healing began. Being alive changed from
being a grim experience into something I revel in
today. That doesn't mean that once in a while I
can't have a brief flashback; but I'm pragmatic about
it: I'm human and I must expect (and accept) the
occasional slings and arrows of outrageous fortune.
The real point is that, thanks to what I've been
taught, I can ride out a rough day and get back to
enjoy life. This book describes the techniques of
change which make that possible.

Now I want to say something very important
about you, and something which I'm certain you
have forgotten. More than anything else you are a
trier, a 'can-do' person. If this were not so, you
wouldn't be reading a book like this. You are not
sitting about doing nothing. Not everybody is
prepared to work for their own happiness, but you
are different. You have not given up. You are, no
matter what you are going through, trying to do
something about it. Whether you are aware of it or
not there is in the heart and centre of you all that
superb courage, that gutsy quality which makes
the pro stand up and fight every time he gets
knocked down. The real pros are not the ones who
never get knocked flat but the ones who keep
coming out again when the intensity of their pain is
crying 'Quit!' Whether it works for you or not (and
only you can make that happen), I can guarantee
that as long as you stay trying, be it sooner or later,
whatever befalls, you are going to make it all the
way. Frankly, I admire people like you because
knowing that you are out there helps get me to my

feet when I run into one I never saw coming. If you can do it, so can I. If I can do it, so can you.

For those reasons I would like you to see this book not as a lesson given by teacher to pupil but as a joint venture between fellow sufferers. It is important for us that it should be so. It is now becoming known that when fellow sufferers make common cause some therapeutic interaction not clearly understood takes place between them which benefits both and often enough quite dramatically. In other words we both have a lot to gain from going these pages together and I know from what I've seen that we'll both reach the end of it as happier and better people.

With problems, we can do one of two things. We can *live in the problem* or *live in the solution*. Living in the problem means dwelling on our depressions and anxieties, telling each other how awful it is and, worse still, feeding each other a spurious sympathy which I know doesn't work because I tried it for long enough. Living in the solution means finding out and doing those things which lead to recovery and happiness so that the problem disappears. I know beyond argument that that's how it works because not alone have I tried it but I know as intimate friends very many people who found the same thing. So the theories and therapies I have picked up from what I've half-read and quarter-understood have no interest for me. I am only interested in what *works* and quite frankly, not particularly interested in why it works. If something works, don't fix it and never waste time asking why. So we'll keep it simple. If an individual unit of earth-moving equipment propelled by the physical exertions of the driver is always called a 'spade,' why call it anything else?

These simple principles of wellbeing and happiness were not worked out by me: I want to be unblushingly candid about that. They are as old as time, but for some extraordinary reason not commonly known. The only claim I make is that I have set them down in a certain sequence and typed them up. But I do want to make dramatic claims for the principles themselves. By gift of God, a little help from our friends and our own willingness to have a go, those of us who try to live by them have become extremely happy and fulfilled people, knowing peace of mind as a fairly constant value and experiencing a joy in living which seems unusual in the world around us. As you will discover, real happiness sometimes consists of being happy because of nothing and in spite of a lot.

The very same miracle of change will take place for you to the extent that you are prepared to give these methods a fair and persistent trial. The only demand made on you is a willingness to try, an open-minded consideration of new ideas, and a determination to throw out old attitudes. If you can go that far, your own experience will convince you far more cogently than anything I could write. So we won't spend much time arguing the case. You will prove it yourself.

Thoreau's observation that the mass of men lead lives of quiet desperation is sadly true. It is true not because it has to be but because most people won't try. Inner peace is not something everyone possesses. It is not easy to acquire; one must work to retain it; but once glimpsed it is worth any effort to find and keep it. It is not a matter of mastering certain concepts as an intellectual exercise. We get well and stay well not by the things we *know* but by the things we *do*. It is a matter of doing, daily doing and lifelong doing. That word *doing* is the secret of the whole system. There is no book or therapy which will work for us without an active deter-mination to *do*, and we've all tried the softer options without getting anywhere. The word *doing* is so important that along every line we write, it will echo with all the monotony of a tolling bell; but if we are not prepared to *do*, let us send not to know for whom the bell tolls.

At times we will be talking about spiritual things. Do not take fright. This is not a religious book and nothing here is in conflict with whatever religious views you may hold.

At other times you may catch me out in repeti-tion. Truth, essential truth, is so utterly simple that we often miss it first time around. A good jazz player punctuates his main theme with repetitive riffs until the beat and statement of what he is playing enters our being and takes it over. That's what makes us swing; that's why we tap our toes. So the repetition is important. Some simple truths are so precious that we dare not risk them by understatement, any more than the jazzman will risk his theme by failing to counterpoint it. So if we've been singing the blues for too long, it's a good thing to change the beat and liven the tempo; and as this book is also about having fun, you'll find now and then that many aspects of life are too serious to be taken seriously. So if in odd moments you find a smile creeping over your face, leave it there. That, I am sure, is how our Creator intended us to live.

Finally, let's get the excess baggage off the flight. Most of the time we'll be cruising above the cloud base, out up there where the sun shines all the time and even the birds can't make the altitude. Fear, doubt, prejudice and pessimism about our chances are the excess baggage which weigh us down and make it harder to get airborne. Let's drop the reservations, the furious thinking and questioning and go with it. Part of the trouble with people like us is that we think too much; we don't let go; we agonise over every detail. Not a free, fun way to live. So for this trip we'll fly it by the seat of the pants, going with it and letting it happen. And we're both going to make it all the way. Now, feet off the brakes and let's roll . . .

think page

Many miracles are performed through human agency.
A certain man bought a house and found that the garden was overgrown with brambles and tumbleweed and an abundant crop of empty beer cans flourished in the switch grass. So he went to work and cleaned it up, cutting back to the soil and reseeding the lawn.
He laid out beautiful flower beds and stocked them fully with shrubs and blossoms which bloomed in a blaze of colour.
A pious old lady passed by and stopped to admire what she saw. 'Isn't God wonderful!' she exclaimed. The man threw her a sharp look. 'You should have seen it when he had it himself,' he said.

2 Getting the facts

If we are going to live in the solution, that is, enjoy life as we were intended to, we had better get the facts about ourselves and life itself. Fact No. 1: we are human. That isn't going to come as a great shock to either of us but do we really know what it means? If we do know have we really accepted it: knowing and accepting something are not the same thing. Fact No. 2: we have to live life. We know that too; but have we ever really thought out and accepted what living life as human beings means?

If we say that we are human, we may be saying more about ourselves than we know; we are saying: that

- *we are flawed*, prone to mistakes and must live with few certainties. Think about it. It's normal and human to have defects of character. It doesn't mean I won't try to improve, but it's OK to find personal shortcomings in myself. It's normal and human to make mistakes, get it wrong at times: it doesn't mean I won't try to get it right, but I'm going to hit the crossbar now and again. It's normal and human not to know the answer at times and be doubtful and unsure. Can we accept all that, that is, accept it deep in the heart and not just up in the head?

- *we are always incomplete*, souls in transit; nobody has it made, but we do have a most extraordinary capacity for growth and change. Think about that. Can we live easily with ourselves knowing that as long as we're alive we'll never have it totally together and we'll always need to keep growing up?

- *we cannot go it alone without* the help of our fellow men and women. Outside Hollywood there are no cool characters who need nobody. So it's OK to be dependent to a healthy extent on the people around us, to have to ask someone to dig us out, give us a bit of advice. Can we accept that?

- something in the heart of us yearns upwards to something we think of as good. So it's very human to wonder from time to time what goes on Up There and want to reach up and find out.

That's what being human means. These rules apply to us and to every human being who ever walked the planet; there are no exceptions. Now, we may have known all that, but do we accept it? Can we sincerely look at ourselves and say it's OK to be human? How do we score on these points? Not until we can embrace all these aspects of ourselves, see them as fully human and normal, can we say that we accept what it means to be human. Maybe that's the first bit of work we have to do. Go over and over it again until we get perfectly at ease with being ourselves, human.

Now the second fact, what about life itself? Do we really know *and accept* what life entails:

1. *Life isn't fair*. The Queensberry Rules it doesn't know about and whether the ref. is looking or not it's going to hit below the belt and jab a thumb in your eye (not all the time of course, but often enough to let you know you've got a fight on your hands).

2. *Virtue has no reward*. People who try to be 'good' so that life will cut them a better deal end up very bitterly disappointed.

3. *Life won't stand still*. In a flurry of apparent contradictions it moves from one unresolved situation to the next. Every time you think you've got the pieces in place, life is going to shake the board.

4. *Life is a mystery* to be lived, loved, enjoyed, exulted in—and not a problem we must solve. Mysteries are not supposed to be solved. There are, of course, many fraudulent fellows who propound answers for other people who receive them gratefully for a time until they discover sadly that they must travel on again and find their own.

So, that's life. But do we accept it? Deep down do we accept that life isn't going to draw a different contract for us and it isn't going to back off, negotiate or go away? Maybe we have to do a little more work coming to terms with these realities. I know I had to. I thought it was a most unreasonable arrangement. I was right.

Now if you add the realities of being human to the realities of life itself you get what the thinking man with the pipe calls the 'human condition'. This is the great sophisticated phrase which keeps the poets and philosophers thinking through the night and the boys in the pubs talking after hours and solving the whole thing. That's why they must keep going back next night.

Now suppose we have never known these things or suppose we have half-known them but never accepted them: what then?

- If we can't accept that we don't know it all and must live in doubt, we'll be terrified of making mistakes and we'll paralyse ourselves seeking certainty.

- If we can't accept our incompleteness, we'll hate ourselves for not being perfect; and because we don't know that we can change and grow, we'll get stuck believing 'This is the way I am and I can't do anything about it.'

- If we can't accept that we need others, we'll lock ourselves into a proud isolation and be incapable of asking for help when we need it. And it's pretty lonely living behind a self-built wall.

- If we can't reach for the stars and shoot for the sky and get to know for ourselves whatever is up there, we must either settle for second-hand beliefs which don't tally with personal experience or ground ourselves on the sterile terrain of materialism and never know ecstasy.

- If we can't accept that life is unfair at times, we'll keep yelling 'foul' while life laughs and does it again: and we'll corrode ourselves with a bitter sense of injustice and self pity.

- If we think that virtue will be rewarded we'll fill our minds with immature ideas of 'deserving' and 'being entitled to' and 'having the right' which all sensible people cut out of their thinking. Life paid its debt the day we were born and after that it's up to you, New York, New York.

- If we can't settle down to live in mystery, we will never know the delight of wonder, the exciting unpredictability of the game and we'll shrivel up baffled and bewildered because we can't work it out for ourselves.

The human condition, that mad mixture of being human and living life, is reality. It excuses no one. That's it. If we can't live with reality we are to a greater or lesser extent neurotic, to use a much misused word meaning out of touch with reality and our surroundings. But forget the scientific jargon, look at the terrible consequences in the ordinary everyday living of life:

We're paralysed by doubt and terrified of mistakes (fear and anxiety), self disgusted by what we are (self-hatred), never knowing we can change (without hope), never daring to reach out to others (lonely and alone) sentenced to creep from day to day in a mad, meaningless world in a nothingness with no purpose (suicidal). In all the great medical textbooks could you hope to find a better description of depression and anxiety?

People like us with tendencies to depression, anxiety, fear and worry are prone to setting ourselves internal standards far above the limitations of the human condition. We impose demands on ourselves which the human person was never intended to meet. We require perfection of ourselves, that we never make mistakes and that we do everything well. We are constantly under stress demanded from within. Being human we can never measure up to our own impossible standards and when we fail as we must we ravage ourselves with self derision and fall into depression. We are running on a terrible treadmill, a merciless sentence pronounced by ourselves. Nothing we ever achieve is good enough for us. Always we have that nagging thought that we should have done it better. We will never be free to be happy until we can integrate a sensible acceptance of our human condition and let ourselves off the hook.

Now we start asking the wrong question. How did I get this way? which is living in the problem. As we will see an examination of our past will be helpful but not now. If I'm sinking in a sea of misery it doesn't matter whether I fell in, was pushed or jumped in. I may well have been deprived of my rubber duck in childhood or harboured repressed sexual designs on Little Red Riding Hood. It doesn't matter. I'm here in the now and I'm going under and the only thing that counts is: Get me out. And as with all human problems we face the only question which matters: What are we going to do about it? Things can get worse or be made worse but they can't get better. They can only be made better. The passive and the active. Passive means letting. Active means just that—*doing*.

However, it is time for a massive injection of hope! We have seen in the realities of the human condition two wonderful and heartwarming messages. First, that the human person is capable of incredible change and growth. Second, that life is intended to be a warm and wonderful experience in which we should exult. These are not fancy theories. These are the realities and to the extent that we doubt or disbelieve them our contact with reality is faulty: we are being neurotic. We must embrace the good news just as firmly as we have accepted the bad news. We are *not* stuck the way we are. We can change. We may not be very hopeful, of course, we've been trying for years without any result. But this time it's different. We are going to use methods that have been tested and tried all over the world and have brought about unbelievable transformations in people with far more difficulties than we have. And we're going to make it. Happiness is our birthright and the promise that we can find peace and fulfilment in our lives is not a theory but the intention of the Creator who established the human condition. If we have lapsed into a negative mind-set, those two great hopes must be the beginning of our transformation. We must reject the notion that life is intended to be an experience of suffering. If other people want to believe that, let them. Let them also live with the consequences.

At this point, let's deal with one or two asides before going further.

What about other people? Where do they fit into our plans for better living? How can we contribute to our own well being by interacting with others?

Did you ever notice that misery is circular and happiness is vertical? If you think that's just a good figure of speech, take a look at a guy with problems and the way he sits. The head is bowed, the chin is in the fist, the shoulders are rounded and the knees are usually drawn up to support the elbow. Jane Fonda could adjust her garter beneath his gaze and he wouldn't blink. Self-absorbed. Circular. By contrast, look at the body language of a fighter who has just won a title or a footballer who has just slammed the ball into the back of the net. The arms are vertical and he's jumping for joy. He's reaching up, punching at the sky with the good of it. Vertical. Putting it all differently: if we can reach out to others we can break out of the circle of misery. Being interested in others is the first way of losing interest in our own misery.

Firstly there are the people we live with, the members of our family. Depressive illnesses of whatever kind can have very painful consequences for others. The inevitable self obsession and withdrawal from others, those classic symptoms of depression and worry, can break marriages, close businesses and bring lovers and friends to sad partings. Neither of us has to play hero and deny that we have suffered much, but we must also see that our illness has caused much sufferings to those around us. Sick people can make others sick. We need have no guilt about that unpleasant fact. We didn't chose to be unwell, and we are not responsible for the illnesses which overtake us, whatever the consequences for others; but we do have an onerous responsibility not just to recover for our own sakes but to create for those whose lives touch ours a better and happier life than ever before. That's what our system is all about. It is not just the negative benefit of being free of pain but the positive blessing of a new and wonderful life for ourselves and those we love. If we can motivate ourselves for others, the inherent self-obsession of depression and its ugly sisters, fear and anxiety, breaks down.

But there is so much more to it than that. When I had less sense I often wondered about the mystery of suffering. Wondering too much is like smoking in bed (very dangerous) but if you're doing nothing better than standing with your hands in your pockets staring out the window it helps to pass the time. Why were we marked out to suffer a cruel illness in the first place? I don't know, candidly, but

I have an opinion which makes sense to me that these burdens were laid upon us not so that we bear them as martyrs and have a bad time but so that we stand them on their head and springboard them to make life better for others who suffer in the same way. Maybe we should not try to solve the intractable problems of life but instead live with them as observers so as to reach an insight which can be passed on to others. If we do that well, we create for ourselves a degree of happiness which we would not have otherwise known. If suffering is all for nothing, it is mean, humiliating and degrading; but if we can fight a battle so that others can win, then all the bad days were a learning process which we can offer to others. Speaking entirely for myself (but hoping that you will find the same thing) I have come to regard what I once resented as a terrible handicap as a great blessing because it has created a quality of life which I could not have known without having been to the wars. So, once we decide to work on recovery not only for ourselves but to pull others out as well, we have set ourselves on the high road to wellbeing by breaking the circle of misery.

Depression and anxiety states often involve significant medical and psychiatric aspects outside our competence. We must confine ourselves to doing those things which only we can do for ourselves—change and grow. There is no therapy which can do this work for us or help us until we develop the self honesty and courage to play our part. Even Cinderella had first to find a pumpkin and a team of white rats. Pumpkins and white rats aren't easy to find. Many people won't try. Psychiatrists often complain that the people who consult them are not prepared to make changes. What they really want is the magic wand treatment while they cling to their old neurotic ways. Like a public phone when the car breaks down, it doesn't work. We must also be careful to leave the psychiatry to the psychiatrists. If we have found it necessary to consult someone, part of our doing involves co-operating fully with the advice given. Psychiatry is a difficult and complex field and life isn't made easier for these compassionate professionals by enthusiastic amateurs invading the pitch. Nothing is availed by our trading symptoms and therapies or regaling each other with our Freudian theories. If after a reasonable trial we find that a particular therapist or treatment doesn't seem to help us we must look around for one which might better suit our particular case. These illnesses are complex. What works for me might not help you. Don't listen to those godawful people who indulge in pseudo-psychiatric discussions or tales of Christy's wife who 'had exactly the same thing as you have and she . . . ' She hadn't. Christy's wife is a unique human being with all the totality of her own temperament, metabolism, physiology and life experience and she isn't you and you aren't her. Nor, might we observe, have you shared the exquisite joy of living with Christy all these years which might conceivably have some bearing on that sad lady's plight.

Now, let's go back to finding the facts.

Here is a simple word which we'll use to replace all the scientific jargon: COMFORTABLE. Don't ask whether we are neurotic or psychotic or disturbed. The question is, are we COMFORTABLE? Comfortable with what?

If we look again to our experience of the human condition we find that as human beings we are involved in three unavoidable human relationships: we must live with our fellow man, with ourselves and with whatever deity exists. Are we comfortable in these three dimensions of reality?

Are we comfortable with God or whatever we think might be up there? We may well be religious, but if we can't be fully at ease with whatever is going on out there where the clouds end we have some work to do. And if any mention of God scares us or fills us with dread then we have a lot of growing up to do.

Are we comfortable being ourselves? Do I enjoy being me—the flawed and fallible human being who doesn't know the answers, can't make it on his own and even with help never has it made? If I am depressed and anxious, fearful and worried, and not particularly delighted to be me, I clearly have some work to do on myself.

Are we comfortable with our fellow man upon whom we must depend for help and support now and again? How do we see others? Do we view them as hostile forces to be competed with and defeated or won over; or as worthy sisters and brothers of the human family with whom we will co-operate for the good of all? If I'm secretly afraid or ill at ease with others, quite clearly I've some work to do in that dimension of reality.

I have to do some reaching and growing:

Upwards to make a comfortable relationship with whatever is up there

Inwards to find a comfortable relationship with myself.

Outwards to find a comfortable relationship with all others.

And suppose we don't? Suppose we are not willing to change and grow, what then?

If we won't grow *upwards*, we must either continue to live with an unfulfilled yearning, or at best settle for whatever others tell us to believe; never to have our own experience.

If we won't grow *inwards* to know and love ourselves as we really, are we must continue to live ill at ease with someone we don't really know, don't like very much and who can't be trusted when the chips go down.

If we won't grow *outwards,* we must travel on as loners, always sheltering behind superficial contacts and touch-and-go relationships, always afraid that others will know us as we really are and never to take our place as equals in the family of man.

Not a good way to be comfortable. Not a fun way to live. Not what this book is about.

Don't think we are the only people in the world who have to work on personal growth. Sooner or later everybody who expects to be happy must confront these issues. The ideally balanced human being doesn't exist outside the pages of the psychology textbooks. Nobody has it made. Here and there you will run into people who seem to have an unbreakable self assurance and think they have it all together because they've never had to deal with a real life crisis. We were all like that once. We knew all the answers and we didn't know there were any questions. Then one day the world fell down and without knowing that we were being favoured we hit rock bottom.

The classic picture of rock bottom is the bearded tramp, a one-time millionaire, drunk and asleep on a coal heap. It isn't necessarily like that. It's different and personal for each of us. It's a bereavement, an serious illness, a business failure, constant unemployment, a terrible injustice, the breakdown of a marriage. The circumstances vary but the feeling is the same. It's that day of ultimate despair, a defeat, a humiliation, a disgrace when we've played out our last card and we've found ourselves helpless, friendless and alone and every truth and certainty we ever had has vanished in a puff and never meant anything. But if it should so happen that you're reading this when you too feel down and out, pause and wonder and give fervent thanks because you may be standing on the threshold of the most beautiful experience you're ever going to know. I know many people including myself who spend a large part of our conscious hours wondering why we were made so fortunate as to reach the fork in the woods and be forced down the less trodden way which made all the difference. Sometimes in life blessings come in heavy disguise; and choices are forced upon us which we wouldn't have had the wit or willingness to make on our own.

In doing what we are about to do we are not embarking on a quick Play the Piano in Seven Days and Amaze your Friends routine: we are entering upon a new way of life. If we expect to transform deeply rooted attitudes in seven days, we may well amaze our friends—but for the wrong reasons. Nothing here promises an easy run; the way is lifelong and uphill. But it's a fascinating journey, filled with new discovery and a growing capacity for personal happiness along a way which gets easier. We will come to know peace of mind and the old negative, depressive thinking will wither and die. Nothing we will learn will excuse us from the occasional bumps and bangs of living but we'll learn to win and lose with grace and dignity and look good doing both. Don't allow pessimism tell you you can't do it. Everybody thinks that, it's part of the condition. The secret is that we tap ourselves into hidden powers, reserves of courage and honesty and you can be certain that in proportion to your willingness to make honest efforts, you're going to find yourself performing way over your known abilities. As we will discover, not alone does this thing work but it keeps getting better.

So now we know. But knowing isn't enough. We grow into happiness not because of the things we know but because of the things we do. And it must be an honest doing. Cop-outs and half measures, trying to cut corners or slide over the hard bits doesn't work. Part of the reason we could never change ourselves before was because we kept trying to do it 'My Way'. We could never face the stark truth that 'My Way' never worked. But this time we know better. And so we come to the first of three exercises, the first step of a way that works.

think page

Some of us need to hit dead centre every
time; the eye in the fly at fifty paces—
right through the middle—in the dark. When
we grow up a little we see that it's OK to have one
end shorter than the other. It's OK to sing off-key.

Anything worth doing is worth doing badly.
We miss a lot of fun by
only doing the things we do well.

So have some fun trying. Don't be afraid
to mess around a little now and then.

3   Growing upwards—God

Fasten your seat belt and hang on to that open mind, for this is the part of the show the dubious punters call the 'God bit.' Nobody likes it. We approach it with fear, boredom, or at best the idea that it's a chapter about religion. It's not. It's about the central reality of the human condition and to the extent that we run and hide or short change it we are slipping back to our old neurotic and childish ways. Putting it in total simplicity, God is Love and that's a truth that the religions of the world have done much to obscure. So let's leave the doctrines and the dogmas and the theology to the theologians and get on with the essential business of growing up to our own personal experience of whatever God exists.

The only thing this chapter asks us to accept is that all reality consists of a mysterious interweave of spiritual forces and unknown things on the one hand and the material things we know about on the other, all presided over by an Ultimate Power or force which can only act in love and which people variously refer to as God, Jesus, Allah, Jehovah, The Lord, The Great Unknowable, The Life Force, Lady Luck, Fate, and dozens of other names we have never heard of. It's a beautiful simplicity and inordinately difficult to write about because the mind keeps interjecting complications which aren't there.

If you are an unbeliever, don't worry. Once you can presuppose that there is some benign and mysterious force out beyond the conscious comprehension of man, it doesn't matter whether that force is located out in the great somewhere or deep in the unknown and hidden resources of the human psyche. Whatever my beliefs may be, nothing gives me the right to say you are wrong. Equally, I ask your tolerance when I express myself in the only way meaningful to me and refer to 'the Father'. Whatever your beliefs or unbeliefs may be, you must substitute whatever concept with which you are most at home. And what happens for you will be just as valid and effective as it is for me.

Don't let religion confuse the issue. Some people are fully at home with their religious upbringing and others have been filled by it with fear, guilt and remorse. If religion assists you towards a personal experience of God, be grateful for it and rejoice in it before all the world. If on the other hand religion obstructs a loving relationship with your Father, do what I did; drop it and run like hell. The God we are talking about is a Loving Father, who can only act in perfect love and doesn't understand guilt, sin, unworthiness, meriting or fear and is infinitely beyond the private ownership of any or all religions. We are talking about a Father who, whatever you may think of yourself or whatever the world may think of you, can only cherish you with a magnificent love, total approval, and delight in your being you—whatever your past—for you are his personal and unique creation. Just wear that in your open mind for a moment. You'll prove it for yourself in due course.

We must stop here and get that concept firmly on board. It's no good nodding our heads and agreeing in our minds. Many of us are riddled with the guilt and self disgust which is part of the depressive anxiety state and any idea that God loves us—or worse, approves of us totally and delights in us—seems like a terrible blasphemy. Many of us have to work very hard to get that idea down out of the head and rooted firmly in the heart. For very many of us it means daring to believe. It's something we have to meditate on constantly until we get it right. Look at it this way: if God can do what he likes he can choose to love us no matter how misguided a choice that may seem to us. Now let's kill off the complications.

We can only talk about God in utter simplicity. Trying to understand God is like staring at the sun in July; do it for long enough and you'll burn your eyes out. Debates about the existence of God can go on for ever and we can set our minds whirling by getting into them. The questions are endless and the answers are circular. Once you start a discussion at all you are right back into the debating society which is no place for those determined to do the doing. Forget the great cosmic questions which keep the philosophers awake at night: 'If God is a loving God why does he allow . . . '. We've all tangled with those questions. If we are determined to *do* and drop the debating, the only answer is that if my Aunt had a rotor she'd be a helicopter and if I knew something like that I'd be God (which is just as nonsensical a piece of nonsense as the thoughts of a flawed human mind which presumes to wrestle with the great cosmic questions known only to God). The purpose of this exercise is to come to know God as a personal experience. Knowing God as a personal experience is not just having a mental concept in the head where we keep the stuff we forget: it is that unshakeable certainty in the gut, where we keep the stuff we remember. We want to create those inner conditions where we are at last able to say that we don't have to believe in God: we know God.

None of us finds God. What happens is we take a firm decision to allow God find us. He is a remarkably polite gentleman. He will not intrude until we ask him sincerely to come and take us over. And he won't do deals. He won't give signs or advance guarantees. Free will means that with no hype or pressure God will leave it to us to call out to him sincerely and entrust ourselves blindly to him. Then, like the father who was watching from afar, he comes running out and we're home at last from the far country. And we can make it as complicated or as simple as we like. There is only one requirement—a willingness to have a go.

Look at our situation, the realities we faced up to:

- We're flawed and fallible and we don't know what's going on, or what makes it all tick.

- We're crippled with fear, anxiety and depression and can just about make it through the day.

- We're tried to handle our own life and we've made bits of it in every direction.

- We're living through a mystery and nobody knows the answer.

- Deep inside every one of us something is aching for something real, and while you can stun it for a time, it keeps coming back and whispering to you when you're trying to think of something else.

- The nearest and dearest to us can't help, for they too are subject to the human condition and must let us down from time to time.

In the light of those realities we take a decision to ask our Father take over the running of our lives. It's that simple.

Putting it at bedrock basic, we opt to believe that if we ask him, a Loving Father who also happens to be the Ultimate Creator and Architect of all things will take over the management of our lives and guide us henceforth in what He knows with infinite wisdom to be for our best interests and well-being. It's called 'handing over'. It's a no-guarantee, no-preconditions, no-hidden-agenda, freefall stunt. The only mechanism that works is a total recognition of our own helplessness and a sincerely intended and honest request. And the greatest difficulty in writing about it is not that it's complicated but that it's so simple that we miss it every time around.

This is not something we think about, discuss, prove, understand, but do. We will always compli-cate it. We can wind ourselves up into a religious fervour and chant all the psalms and nothing will happen. We can sign on for a comprehensive renewal of religious observance, repentance for sin, and nothing will happen. We can spare ourselves the feverish devotion. We ask sincerely. We concede absolute defeat. We do it and watch what happens. And we will then have our own evidence that we are deeply loved and cherished by God himself with all the intensity of a laser beam as if nobody else in the world existed.

Don't load it with difficulties which don't exist. Don't get too dismayed by your inability to be sincere. The prodigal son wasn't coming home to be a good boy. He was coming home because he had blown all the bread and he hoped his father would give him a job feeding the pigs. Remember too that contrary to all the sermons the prodigal son never made it home. He didn't have to. His Father had been keeping watch for him and came running out. All the young man had to do was make a start. Do the doing. Take the action. It was the Father who finished the job. It is exactly the same for us.

Our pride and egotism is not going to like this arrangement. We think we will become nobodies, puffs of smoke, no personal initiative. Don't you believe it. God will always expect us to set our goals, go for them, give every situation our best shot. But we let God work out the results. Why? Because he can see what's coming round the next corner and we can't.

God comes to us and takes us over as his own because we have lowered the barriers of pride and egotism and let him. He does so not because we are saintly people or 'worthy' or have 'merited' him but because he has chosen to love us and that choice is fixed. So we can spare ourselves the embarrassment of pass-the-plastic-basin piety and settle down to enjoy life, letting the Father work his wonders through us.

What exactly happens? There are innumerable kinds of spiritual awakenings which happen either in a 'hot flash' experience or in a dawning awareness that God has possessed and transformed us; and one is as valid as the other. God discloses himself to us in a personal imagery and language which only we understand fully and which we cannot communicate clearly to anybody else. At first this can be very frustrating, the closest thing to being in love and wanting the world to know and yet being unable to give a very coherent account of what has taken place. After a while we learn to accept that we can't describe it and we give up trying. This is no Sunday morning high which wears out by lunchtime; it is something very definite which doesn't go away when Monday comes. It effects either immediately or gradually a transformation in our personality which other people seem to notice before we do. God establishes with each one of us a uniquely personal relationship but one which we can share to some degree with others who have been through the same thing which enables us to form some consensus about the nature of God and how He works. This is why we are able to pass on the message to each other and offer some guidance in times of doubt. And all we have to do then is keep trying to develop that relationship with God by daily conversations with him.

In practical terms, how do we hand ourselves over to God each day? Everyone has their own best way of doing it but generally we start at the first waking moments of the day by reminding ourselves that we are no longer living alone, trying to solve our own problems, and that everything we need to live through that one day is fixed and arranged. We have linked ourselves into an unstoppable power which is infinitely loving and deeply interested in all our doings. God can only act in love for our happiness and wellbeing. We must be careful here. We all have very set ideas about what is best for us and pride and self-will will always insist on their way. We will find ourselves praying that our plans will come to pass, our dreams come true and our arrangements work out the way we think they should. That is not what handing over is about. Handing over means that we pray not for certain events to happen or not to happen but that we be given the serenity to live happily with whatever situation arises, knowing always that the Father knows what he is doing, has the longer view and better ideas than we have. Once we are clear about that (and it only comes with practice) we are content to do our best and let things happen as they will. When our own plans blow up we don't get too upset because we know the Father is running our lives. In all our moments of doubt and difficulty we need only ask one question: 'Who runs my show?' If God is running it, let him. That is exactly what handing over means. Just because some problem seems unanswerable to us it does not mean that God is equally confused. As we fall asleep at night we review our day and hand it all over again, including all the times we did badly and missed the mark. The essence of this exercise is action, consistent and daily. We don't think or theorise. We do it.

In this new way of living there is only one sin and that is to give up. Perfection isn't on and God did not create us as perfect. The essence of being human is that we are unfinished business. We never have it made and always need to keep travelling on. We work for progress and nothing more and we must be calmly content to do it badly at times, make a lot of mistakes and at times fall into moments of furious rebellion and all the lusts, selfishness, pride and stupidity of the human condition. Far from being surprised or disappointed with us, God expects all this. He created us as human, fallible and imperfect. He has chosen to love us. None of our human antics are going to make him change his mind. He can't change his mind. How do we know? Because being infinitely wise, God can't get a better idea. He gets it right first time. So in so far as mistakes are concerned, we can put away the big stick and stop being so hard on ourselves.

Now, what has all this to do with anxiety states and depression? The daily awareness of being loved by God has a profound affect on our temperament. As we progress, we acquire an inner peace because we are learning that there are many things we no longer have to worry about. Old anxieties die away, a quiet inner confidence replaces the attention-seeking self-importance, and the experience of being loved edits out of us the self-disgust and self-hatred so closely linked to depression. We begin to develop a proper self-esteem, and, freed of many of the old inner tensions, we can start to look around and enjoy life. We begin to be fascinated by simple things we missed out on before, and, as we will see later on, our new attitudes have a most beneficial effect on the way we deal with other people. We seem to be tapping into reserves of courage, self-honesty and an instinctive wisdom which is quite clearly not our own. We find ourselves able to handle with ease situations and people which used to baffle and upset us in the past. We undergo a growing awareness that there is a lot more going on than we can see and touch or understand with the mind. We grow comfortable with mystery, no longer troubled by what we cannot foresee or understand. We get a hunch for right timing, and an ability which can startle others to be unconcerned when things look very serious indeed. We know that we are not running the show and we don't need to know very many answers.

What about practical everyday living?

1. FEET ON THE GROUND: Leading a life on spiritual principles does not excuse us from the human condition or from the worldly realities. A days work has to be done, bills have to be paid and we stop at red traffic lights. Jesus himself refused to do a circus stunt from the pinnacle of the temple on the promise that his Father would bear him up. Beware of the 'Lord will provide' merchants who are cousins of those who expect psychiatrists to wave magic wands. The Father will certainly look after us in the most wondrous ways but only after we've done our human best and handed over. We still need to use our talents and make our own decisions after seeking guidance from the Father and availing of the human advisors he has placed at our disposal. We will get the guidance we ask for, but very often the Father will remain silent for a time so that we will have the humility to turn for help to those around us. But feet on the ground at all times. 'To hell with your philosophy: who pays the rent?'

2. GET A GUIDE: It is not wise to make spiritual journeys alone. Self will and pride never fall asleep and time and again we rationalise to pretend to ourselves that our own selfish plans are the inspirations of God. Find some priest or

minister or some person you can trust who lives by these principles, and talk to him or her regularly about your progress. Don't be too worried about finding the right person. Once we make the effort the Father brings to us the people we need to guide us. When the pupil is ready the master appears.

3. MIND OUR OWN BUSINESS: Just as we agreed to leave the psychiatry to the psychiatrists, we leave the theology to the theologians. The religious controversies of the day and the great metaphysical questions are not the business of people intent on doing. If we rest our lives in the hands of a Father who knows all things, for what do we need to know anything?

4. PRAYER: Here's a tough one. Should we pray for the things we want? I don't know the answer and I can only offer you a personal opinion. The answer is no. Either my Father is running the show or I am. If my Father is running the show I can't see the point in using a flawed human intellect even to suggest to an Infinite Wisdom what ought to be done, and even the 'if it be thy will' bit compromises an absolute acceptance. For peace and serenity and the ability to hang in hard I ask endlessly, but I leave it there, and things work out far better for me than if I had scripted my own show in the first place. Nobody, but nobody, tells Sinatra how to sing; but the whole world seems down on its knees telling God what to do.

However, there is a little more to it than that. While writing this section, I underwent a period of doubt about my career options and the financial contraints which ensue when working as a full time writer were biting hard—coin of the realm was in short supply and I could only describe a pound note from memory. As a result of praying for guidance, I met a priest by accident who was a good listener and I posed the question to him. He was emphatic that the Father is the Father and should be approached with confidence for the things we need to live our lives fruitfully. He also discerned in my attitude an unformed fear that God had been more than good already and should not be troubled further and/or that money was too sordid a topic to be mentioned. I was, he pointed out, shrinking God down to my own humanity. I still feel that the less prayers of request said the better, for requests tend to compromise absolute acceptance but there is no use in seeking guidance and then second-guessing it and I now feel that there can be times when all human ingenuity fails and it is right and proper to turn to a heavenly Father and request specific material help. There is, of course, a world of difference between making a request and an arrogant demand for a specific answer to be delivered to a deadline. In any event, I thanked the good priest for his guidance which was most emphatically given and went home to extend this page by the addition of this paragraph, lest I gave advice which my Father would repudiate. The less trouble when I go home the better.

5. LET GOD PRAY TOO: Could it ever be that God might like to pray to us? Take time out to slouch round the place with your hands in your pockets, thinking about nothing at all but conscious that

you are your Father's child. It's amazing what you can pick up and the peace which will come to you. All too often what passes for prayer is nothing more than a mental racket which blots out the voice of God.

6. WANTS AND NEEDS: The Father will provide the things we need for our wellbeing so we can afford not to get too worried, come in second best some of the time and stop trying to outmanoeuvre our fellow man and beat him to the punch. Our wants are rarely provided for and the more we look back from the rising ground of hindsight the happier we become about that. Some of the things we wanted most earnestly would have destroyed us.

7. THE SPIRITUAL LIFE: This way of life involves no sugar-coated sanctity or pious posturing. It's eyeball to eyeball reality all the way, and if we are serious about growing up and becoming real people we wouldn't have it any other way. Days will come when your humanity will rise up and beat you flat and you can see no progress at all. It doesn't matter a whit. A lot of progress is unseen and made when we think we are making none at all. Don't get disturbed when you seem to do it badly after a period of doing very well. These are the safety catches which remind us of our need to stay home with the Father and not go wandering off again to the far country thinking we can handle it. No mistake matters except to give up; the only sin there is.

We don't have to explain or justify our way of life to anybody. Nor have we any authority to go crusading in the world or telling people how to live. God doesn't need personal bodyguards or public relations officers. If somebody wants to share in what we have been given, we must go down the line to pass the message. That does not mean foisting our beliefs on everybody or angling every conversation round to spiritual things. There are enough gurus driving Cadillacs without our going into business to jam the traffic. We will meet from time to time suave and sophisticated people who can be quite condescending to those who believe in God. Some of them are playing games; others are sincere and good people whose life experience has satisfied them that there is no God. Live and let live. That is a belief they are perfectly entitled to hold without any superior comment from us. Whether they accept it or not they are just as important and cherished by God as we are. But we don't let others do our thinking for us. And we don't explain or apologise. We call our own shots by kind permission of nobody. But we keep an open mind at all times. We are not any more special to God than anybody else, and anybody we meet can teach us something.

Don't hang back on this one. Go to it like a stunt man. In the old days before they started using gelatine, a stunt man would crash through a window by running hard at it. If he hit it hard enough he would crash through without a scratch. If he hesitated he could slice himself to pieces. In a certain sense this exercise is one which God does, not us. All we need going in is unreserved willingness, a decision to persevere, and sincerity. Once we put in our best effort—however weak and confused that may be—God himself supplies the shortfall. But when it happens for you—which it will-you will undergo the most moving and beautiful experience of your life and the in depth, healing transformation of all that you are will begin. Have no misgivings about your chances. The sad, worthless feeling that God cannot love you or disapproves of you is part of the depressive illness, a mean, thieving, destructive lie. It is the Father who does the works and we don't have to make our own progress. And we don't have to die to see God.

think page

Most people take a holiday every year.
Wealthy people take two or more.
Wise people take one every day.

Find yourself a quiet place along a river bank or a shaded walk in a park, somewhere peaceful in an art gallery, a church or a library. Go there every day for half an hour of tranquillity.

Don't tell anybody where it is. Just sit there and slip the world off your shoulders and listen to yourself without thinking. You have often kept worse company.

Know that you are the one-off, unique creation of God. You were not an accident, a whim of fate. You were blue-printed, thought out, carved in the mind of God before the outer edge of time began. God does not design junk.

That makes you a very special person, entitled to your own love and respect. Sit there and think about that until it goes deep inside you.

When you get back you'll find that the world went on quite well without you; the sun didn't fall out of the sky. So, promise yourself faithfully that you'll do it again tomorrow.

4 Growing inwards—me

Worry, anxiety and depression can send our self-esteem crashing through the floor, making us feel guilt-ridden and ashamed of ourselves for no good reason. It is important therefore that we settle ourselves with a secure self-image based on fact. We are not going to be happy with ourselves unless we can know, accept and love ourselves, not as the super people we once believed we should be, but as ourselves, wobbles, weaknesses and all. And that's the work we do now. Getting to know ourselves. Growing In. Getting comfortable with me. And the good news is that without realising it we have already done a fair part of the work for in the previous exercise we have come to realise that we are the cherished children of God himself and as such people of an awesome importance.

Some people think it is conceited to think well of ourselves and that to love ourselves is selfish and wrong. They think that humility means shooting ourselves in the foot and running ourselves down. This is dangerous nonsense. Given our status as children of God it is realistic and proper to love and respect ourselves, and it only becomes conceitful when we think that we are better or closer to God than others. It is essential to our balance and wellbeing to be aware of our innate goodness. This is not egotism. We are not the authors of our own nobility; that is a birthright from God the Father and no temporal authority can take it away. We are entitled to our own self respect and to the respect of others. We will see later how exactly the same thing applies to everyone else.

If we can come to accept and love ourselves as we are (with every fault and defect we have), we can get very comfortable with ourselves and come to see that we are the best friend we have. But if we are to know ourselves truly we must begin the life-long and most exciting journey of self-discovery. In this exercise we will be scraping away the accumulated layers of self-deception of the unexamined years, dropping the masks and giving up the games all people play. Any actor will tell you that playing a role burns off enormous emotional energy. Some of us have spent all of our lives on stage, being all things to all men and wondering why we feel so drained and washed out all the time. If we can do the work of self confrontation, find out who we are and accept that, we will shed a crushing burden and experience a very real sense of freedom. This work cannot be avoided or shoddily done. Until we face up to being ourselves, we will always be at odds with ourselves and ill at ease with others. As with anything else in life which looks complicated, we break it down into separate phases. We have three things to do.

1. We conduct an indepth self examination, list our strengths.and weaknesses and the wrongs we have done.

2. We make a detailed disclosure of our findings to God and one other human being.

3. As an ongoing daily exercise we conduct a brief review of ourselves every night and put right as soon as we can any wrong we may have done.

It is at this stage most of us pull back, reluctant to go on. A self-examination seems little trouble but showing our hand to somebody else is too much for our pride. Indeed we might well discover much in ourselves which it might seem prudent to keep private. And that is exactly why it doesn't work. If we are to be comfortable with ourselves, we must fit ourselves into the reality of who and what we are, and we cannot expect to be at ease if we are working to preserve an image. Fitting ourselves into reality involves a deflation of the ego, a cutting of ourselves down to size. In these steps what we are really doing is taking ourselves down a peg or two, because many people who suffer from anxiety and depression are really suffering from the stress of trying to live up to some superman expectation of themselves which has no basis in reality. The more we hang back from this exercise, the more certain we may be that our ego is badly over-inflated and urgently in need of chopping down. If we cop out of this one we will never grow up and we'll go on playing games for ever. Not a good way to be comfortable.

Take heart. We all find that once a start is made the fear and evasiveness die away and we seem endowed with more candour and objectivity than ever we thought we had. Pride is always a coward. It will always scream quite loudly and make noise in the beginning but once it is confronted and down-faced, it will slink away.

Listing the wrongs we have done is the easiest part of the work. We know well what our wrong doings have been—too well. But a list of historical wrongdoing isn't enough. If we are to know ourselves what we need to find out is not so much what we have done wrong but why? What are the triggers of my defects? Why do I become blazingly angry in certain situations? Why do I so dislike being contra-dicted or being found to be mistaken? What defects in my character are driving me in a certain way? Why do I bitterly resent certain people—what is it in me which they seem to threaten? Am I so tensed up inside that I lose my temper easily when things go wrong? Why am I so tensed up? What crazy standard of perfection am I trying to live up to that I can never let myself off the hook? If I make a mistake in front of others do I feel awfully ashamed and embarrassed or do I laugh at it? Am I so perfec-tionist in my head that I get upset if the tiniest thing is out of place? Am I so unable to control myself that I have a driving need to control everything around me? If I am constantly being untrue to myself to impress others, why this deep need for the good opinion of others? Am I good to people because I love them or because I want to take them over and run their lives? Questions, questions. Let's cut this right down to the root: go for pride every time.

If we can recognise our own pride, seventy-five per cent of our work is done in one surgical stroke, because pride is crosswired into several other human failings which we can dig up at the same time. What is anger but pride thwarted? What is fear but pride anxious for itself? What is self pity but pride in tears? But of all the vices, pride is incredibly difficult to recognise in oneself. It will always cop a plea, that is, plead guilty to a lesser offence to evade detection. It will double-blind and masquerade as virtue, high standards, conscientiousness, the pursuit of excellence, and most of all, it will kick viciously against discovery. Of all the defects it will deny itself to the last and say it is not there; but if you can grab it by the tail, be prepared for screams of protest, and, as you drag it out, be also prepared to be cast into a fit of depression: oh, no, of all things, let it not be pride! Put me down for lust, anything, but not pride! And as usual, once it is confronted it loses its power. Scribble the word on a piece of paper, scrawl a circle round it and sign your name. That's me. Rigid with it. But now it's pegged out in the open where I can get a clean shot at it and from now on I know it's there.

It's obvious from what we have been saying that an in-depth personal examination is much more than twenty minutes in an armchair thinking about it. Prolonged or constant introspection is not healthy, but at this point of our recovery it is exactly what we require. For a time a dedicated self-obsession must be the order of the day. Consider what we are doing. We are setting ourselves up for a new way of living. We are going to the roots of ourselves and dragging up entrenched attitudes, many of which we don't even know we have. We are digging up the buried secrets, opening up the cupboards to find the skeletons, surfacing the hidden garbage and preparing to throw it all overboard so that we can be free. Gradually we build up a composite picture of who we are. We must be equally factual about our strengths and assets. There is much about us which is fine and good and we come out with a very unbalanced picture if we don't list the credit side of the ledger as well. If we have any sense of humour at all a true self portrait will provide much to amuse us for we will find that most of us are a crazy mixture, the depraved saint, the wise fool, the honest liar, the skilled incompetent, the clown in tears.

Now we can accept and love ourselves with an affectionate tolerance for the good and bad people we are. We stop taking ourselves so seriously and get down off the cross. We can have a bit of fun from now on observing our own antics. We can open up to others and be quick to admit our faults. We are doing something about them. Now that we *know* better we'll *do* better.

Now comes the real ego buster—reporting our findings. But is it really that difficult? Of course not. If I totally accept myself as the person I am, it does not perturb me unduly to share myself with you. On the other hand, if I am still playing games and anxious to pretend to be other than I am, I won't enjoy you finding out what I really am. But like it or not, business is business and if we are sincere in our intention to do the doing we will not put this off. To the extent that we find ourselves copping out, we can be sure that pride is still active within, smokescreening plausible excuses to put this off. Now, who do we go to?

If we have been serious in our work so far, we have already found ourself a spiritual guide who knows what we are trying to do. If we prefer to deal elsewhere (and we might well wonder why) we find ourselves some mature and discreet person who knows how to listen—a friendly priest, our family doctor, a close and objective friend or maybe a good psychiatrist we have come to know. Some of them make superb confidants. They know when to listen and when to question and they'll keep us from flying too high or too low on the glide path. The real tester: will he shut up and listen? If we find ourselves with some gameplayer who just wants to hear our first sentence so that he can rumble on for hours on an ego trip, tell him the White House is on the line and we have to go. The work we are doing is far too important for us to waste our time with some plastic person who doesn't know his own reality. What's his style? Is he some pipe puffing helper who sits looking wise and glancing thoughtfully at the ceiling every few minutes to read his notes or is he real enough to come out of hiding behind his desk and sit knuckle to knuckle and knee to knee, chuckling occasionally as he recognises some of his own off the wall antics in what we have to tell him? Does he tell you things— nippy little quotations from *Reader's Digest*—or ask you some tough questions? Will he keep you on balance and prevent you from being too hard or soft on yourself? Is he a real main line person or some armchair philosopher who likes abstract discussions about the human condition—apt quotations thrown in free of charge? These are the things we take into account in selecting some-body to help us.

The sense of freedom, born-again vitality, from a thorough job well done is indescribable. At last we can say: I know who I really am and so does somebody else. The childhood traumas and secret hurts are all out, old ghosts fade in the sunlight of reality and a great stone which we never knew was there has rolled off our heart. We see now with total clarity why this work was so essential to our wellbeing and progress. We also see that it was far easier than we thought and all our fears were only the blackmailing of pride. The real you can stand up. Take a bow and wave to the world. You've done a hell of a job.

But there we leave it. The introspection and self analysis is over and we must get on with living, flying it on the automatic pilot and doing no more than glancing at the instruments in our nightly review. Don't fixate on a particular defect. Work quietly, do your best and let the progress happen. We don't in fact get rid of our own defects and there isn't too much point in worrying about them. As we go on some of them will be taken away quite mysteriously, all will diminish, but some will be left to us to remind us of our humanity. We will always be human, and once in a while we will turn in a bad performance. Mistakes, far from being setbacks, are learning opportunities. As we saw the only mistake that matters is to stop trying.

Now, here's a little story I think you should know: Old lady takes her cat to the vet to be neutered. She's getting on in years, she needs her sleep and she can no longer endure the howls and yowls of the tom's midnight amours. The vet applies his skill, the proper fee changes hands and off she goes, the disendowed cat lying bewildered and semi-anaesthetised in the bottom of her shopping basket half thinking to himself that if this is somebody's idea of a joke, funny it ain't. Within the week she is back, purple with indignation.

'Ye robber! You took my money and you didn't do it right!'

'What do you mean, Madam?'

'Sure, isn't he still gone half the night and the screeching and howling of him on the coal shed is only pure horrid.'

It was the vet's turn to explode.

'Dammit, Ma'am, did you think I could cut the idea out of his head?'

Moral: we don't change overnight.

think page

Some years ago three Americans crossed the Atlantic in a hot-air balloon; they landed somewhere in France I think. They were all Air Force colonels or something like that; guys about my own age—old enough to know better.

One of them was asked in an interview why he did it. I've never forgotten his answer. 'I try to do something daft every day.'

We were all like that once. Maybe we've let too many years go by. It's a po-faced world, of course. But do yourself a favour. Try to do something daft once in a while.

5 Growing outward— our fellow man

We now take the last of the hard, ego-breaking steps to straighten out our past and then we can concentrate on getting to know our brothers and sisters of the human race and joining the human family. What remains to be done?

In listing our wrongdoings we will have noted that there are people we have injured and dealt with unjustly. We cannot have peace of mind until we list these people, become willing to make amends, and go and do it. What in fact we are doing is plucking out of our conscience any festering guilt in relation to others which makes it impossible to live our lives in serenity. In taking this action (as in no other) we need a high degree of timing, prudence and close consultation with a chosen guide.

Firstly, irrational guilt is always part of a depressive, anxious mind-set. Our purpose is to right the wrongs we have done, and unless we have lead the lives of master criminals our list will not be a long one. (There is no need to include those with whom we just may have had cross words; or those unfortunate personality clashes which put neither party in the wrong but are a sad part of normal living.) Secondly, there are certain situations which should remain buried in the past, for we have no right to seek our own peace of mind by disclosing things which take peace of mind from others. There are also those people in the past, some dead and gone, who were part of an oil-and-water, chalk-

and-cheese situation (some of these might well be family members). We must accept as a fact that we cannot get on with everybody we meet, nor should it worry us. Nothing obliges us to maintain contact with those who cannot understand us: that is their problem. Other peoples' approval or disapproval should become a matter of indifference. But in all these areas of doubt we must pray for guidance and follow the advice of our spiritual guide. We must be absolutely certain that we are not copping out and calling it prudence, because every time the ego is threatened, pride will rationalise immediately. Growing real is hard work, and anything which involves cutting the inflated ego down to size will kick. Prudence, guidance and action are the watchwords.

Having reflected on our past, taken advice and made our list, we make personal contact with the people involved. With most people all that is required is a sincere apology. With some there may be a question of restitution or amendment as well. We make a factual admission of our wrong and then make immediate arrangements to rectify it. There is no need to grovel or lose our dignity, but we do well to keep our excuses to ourselves and just deal with the reality of the situation. We must be very careful of our attitude. We have not come to be forgiven, to be thought well of, to reopen old battles, least of all to seek an apology in return from people who might have been at fault as well. Our purpose is to clean up our own act and not anybody else's. The way people respond is none of our business. (In fact, most people are far kinder and more understanding than we think and many a bloodstained hatchet has been buried on these occasions.) What matters is the sincerity of our action. If somebody wants to regard us as an enemy, they are the ones with the problem. We will regard no one as an enemy, and we will no longer have our attitudes dictated by what others do.

Now, have we any more mopping up to do? If we have not been well, it is quite possible that we have let our affairs get out of order. Almost inevitably our financial and taxation matters need some tidying up if we are to be at peace. Because we tend to be conscientious people we are more than anxious to put everything right—by Thursday. Life is not like that. We are doing our best, it is true, but we must learn to suspect flick-of-the-wrist options which appear to provide immediate answers. We invariably find that having set up some brilliant stunt to deal with our money worries and put it through with a most commendable dispatch, we have made matters unbelievably worse. We may also have gone to our bank manager and with the best will in the world agreed to repay our loan at a rate far in excess of our means. All we have succeeded in doing is imposing even further pressures upon ourselves which we can't take. Not a good way to be comfortable. So, how should we go?

The bottom line rule is: we tell the truth. If our affairs are complex enough, we go to the proper professional advisers and put the cards on the table—face up and all of them. And we leave the worrying to the professionals. That is their job. We then act on whatever advice we are given. That is our job. On the other hand, if we can manage without professional help, we go to our bank and our creditors and do exactly the same thing. We tell the truth. Bankers and business people are realists.

They respect truth and deal reasonably with it. Sensible arrangements can be agreed so that the rights of all parties are respected in a manner within everybody's competence. No banker or creditor is interested in listening to romantic promises, however well intended. This particular operation may hurt our pride (always an excellent idea), but we must learn to accept that just as other people make financial and business misjudgments, so do we. We don't do other people's thinking for them. We have no right to assume that other people are less reasonable than we are. Bankers, tax inspectors and creditors are reasonable human beings. That's why they have got where they are. They have no wish to be vindictive, but if we insist in misleading them with halftruths and evasions we have only ourselves to thank if the negotiations take a sour turn. The bald truth frankly spoken has a magic effect on the hearers. Many of us who went through the 'cards up' operation found that we were treated with more respect, co-operation and goodwill than if we had traded through the years with no problems at all. 'The truth shall set you free,' said Jesus who, if memory serves us aright, used to know one or two tax guys himself.

When we reach this stage and provided our work has been honestly and thoroughly done, we cross an important line, for we have now taken every practical step to put ourselves into a comfortable and balanced relationship with God, ourselves and our fellow man. We have tried to cut ourselves down to size, mop up the wrongs of the past and settle ourselves with a serene conscience, and there isn't one person out there whom we can't meet and look in the eye. From now on all our efforts are directed to keeping ourselves in balance and continuing to grow real. And part of that growth involves joining the human family as equal to all and better than none and growing outwards to accept, understand and love others. We have already started this process. Now let's apply what we have learned of the human condition to our fellow man.

We have seen that we ourselves are the chosen, unique, cherished and intensely loved children of a divine Father and that this gives us an extraordinary dignity and entitlement to respect and self respect. Now we apply exactly the same principles to those around us. We need to be quite sure that we have assimilated this concept at deep level. It is not an intellectual platitude for a political speech. We must make it a living reality which colours all our attitudes and actions. This is not easy. It applies to people we don't like, people who annoy us and people who wrong us. We must work constantly to make this attitude a reflex response to everybody. There are no write-off people and there are no top people, and each one's innate dignity is the imprint of God and not something we graciously concede.

But each one is human and subject to all the limitations we talked about. Are we prepared to see that? The other fellow is entitled as a human to:

- Be wrong at times.

- Let us down at times.

- Be tired, bloodyminded and confused.

- See situations from a unique perception entirely different from our own.

- Fail to measure up to his own standards.

- Be victim to his own inner pains and hidden pressures which we know nothing about.

If we have forgiven our own sins—and we won't be real until we do—and accepted our shortcomings with a tolerant shrug, can we let the other fellow off the hook as well? And if not, why not?

And here's a tough one, maybe the toughest one of all:

- Exactly the same applies to those we love and live nearest to. They too are entitled to be wrong, have their faults, let us down at times and fail to come through. Are we real enough to understand and accept that and cut out the childish grievances?

Now here's a crash course in interpersonal relationships in a few paragraphs. If we can make these the basis of our attitude to the world, all the rest is theory, excess baggage.

1. Most people do the best they know, and when they know better they will do better. Those who come on as rude and hostile, the main chance players and the manipulators, do that because it's the best way they know of handling the situation. How do we know? Well, what were we like before someone grabbed our sleeve and taught us better ways?

2. People who treat us sourly are often unaware that we're there. What they are really doing is expressing an inner pain which has nothing to do with us.

3. People will usually respond to us with exactly the same measure of friendliness and courtesy we extend to them. Give hassle, get hassle. You can often break into some cross-faced divil by a head-on attack of friendliness. Forget the How to Win Friends and Influence People tactics, manipulation by any other name stinks just as badly. How real are we?

4. We may go where we please, but we'll never meet anybody worse than ourselves. Think hard about this one. We may well meet people sicker, madder than ourselves, people who have not been given this code to live by, people carrying crosses which would break us in two—but worse? If we had been subject to the same influences and pressures—would we be any better?

5. There's a theory that the defects we most dislike in others are the very ones we refuse to acknowledge in ourselves. Theory or truth? Now there goes one to keep us staring at the ceiling in the small hours.

6. Who are our heros? Do we look up to headliners, sports stars, entertainers, public figures, and never see that behind closed doors in any village or town there's enough heroism going on to blow the roof off the media. So if it's heroes we want, knock next door. Stand that on its head. Do we ever remember that the famed, the wealthy and the powerful are just ordinary people moving it along from day to day the best way they know? Live and let live applies all over town.

7. Once in a while the ball hops our way and we pull a stunt and get the credit. We forget that the

stroke was the joint operation of many unseen people around us and that the concept of personal achievement might just be one more myth.

Shake those seven points like dice and what do you get? That everyone, rich and poor, the famed and unknown are our brothers and sisters of the human race and there is only one thing about anybody which is any of our business. Is he comfortable? And if he isn't, can we fix it? And if he is and we're not, have the humility to ask him how he does it.

And as we grow to become fascinated with the wellbeing of others a very magical thing happens for us. The aching ego where all our problems lie shrinks until we break out of the circle of misery and straighten into the vertical of happiness. And because our self value is invested in inner things, we stop trying to conform, impress, keep up with the Joneses or allow others define what we should be and how to be it. And if we have no longer a need of recognition, praise and approval, we can move out of ourselves to others in a spirit of brotherhood and co-operation; and the old competitive, envious attitudes die. We know that our needs are provided, and we have no demands or expectations to impose on others. We study each situation we get into to see what contribution we can make without wanting anything back. Everything we need has been fixed and arranged.

Now, how can we become fully paid up members of the human race, genuine brothers and sisters in the human family? It is much simpler than boy-scouting around not minding our own business, helping old ladies across the street and wondering why the same admirable convention doesn't apply to young ladies as well. One of the deepest needs people have is not our grand-stand generosity or high-handed 'helping' but to be listened to and understood. Totally accepting listening is inordinately difficult, and few people do it well. We have two eyes and two ears but only one mouth, and nature itself supplies the clue that we listen four times as much as we talk; the eyes, contrary to received truth, being listening devices as well. What makes it difficult is that we hear the words but not what is being said because half the time we are listening to a million fancy theories going round in our brain all bursting to get an airing. We are not listening at all, of course, we are busy writing our notes and waiting for an opening to show that we are much more than a pretty face. If somebody dignifies us by asking us to listen to them—and that doesn't come too often as a formal request but quite often as a casual remark—the whole basis of the encounter is equality of humani-ty and sharing. It's his show, not ours. We don't count. All our advice, our snappy stories and 'If I were you' admonitions matter not at all. It is very important here to understand the 'helper' syndrome and be everything the helper is not. The helper has no real interest in the other person. What the helper is relating to all the time is his own technique, ability to get 'results' and give answers; being wholly unable to relate to anybody as an equal he will keep himself surrounded by unmarried mothers, alcoholics, battered wives or just about anybody vulnerable enough to feed his illusion of superiority. He is endlessly sniffing the ground for someone with a problem. Unless we want to become 'helpers', our total concentration must be on the need of the other person to express his pain, and whether we can come in with an answer or not has nothing to do with it. Our answer doesn't count. What counts is the creation of a caring, accepting atmosphere where someone in trouble can talk out their pressures and work their way round to their own truth. In essence there is little more to it than being able to communicate tacitly the sincere message 'I give a damn.' In fact our helping of others is not an act of the ego, but once in a while and usually without our being aware of it we are used as an instrument of peace and it's a good, warm feeling to be around when it happens.

think page

We move from one self-deception to another, peeling them as layers of an onion. And we reach the point of saying: this is the real me. At last I know who I am. We go on for a year or two and then we say, I thought I knew, but now I do. This is the real person I am. When it happens again and again through the years, you learn to smile a little at yourself, learning at last that because you're still alive there is some unfinished business to transact.

But if through a million incarnations everything false was stripped away, what would emerge? Could it be God Himself?

6 Getting it together

Let's see what we have been doing and draw together the loose threads. When we met at the beginning we were having a bad time. Whatever the details our basic problem was that we were living neurotically—not responding in clear contact with reality. We substituted the concept of being 'comfortable' and we found that we were not comfortable with God, ourselves or our fellow man. So we started to take active steps to grow in these three dimensions, upwards to know God, inwards to know ourselves, and outwards to know our brothers and sisters of the human family.

That took some doing. We had to open our minds, abandon a lot of prejudice and old ideas which had been holding us back, cut out a lot of cop-outs and swallow some unpalatable truths about ourselves. Then we discovered something else, something exciting; that no matter how difficult the way ahead appeared to be, once we made an honest beginning the reality was never as hard as it looked, and we found in ourselves unsuspected reserves of self-honesty and courage. Something beyond our known capabilities was working for us. To face up to ourselves is the hardest thing of all, and if we have come this far we deserve a bit of credit and are entitled to think well of ourselves. We have not walked an easy road. While it is true that the courage and humility we need to go the distance are gifts given to us, there is always one preliminary requirement which is distinctly our own and without which even God himself cannot intervene—and that is our own willingness. Nothing is possible without that. The happiness and wellbeing of this way of life is not open to those who need it; only to those who want it. But once our willingness is on the table, all is possible. Whatever our shortfall in trust, humility, honesty and courage, once we have the willingness to make a start, the tools we need are supplied on the job. The power behind us is infinitely superior to the obstacles in front of us. But we did the doing. We turned to God, sorted ourselves out and began to relate to our fellow man in a spirit of service and co-operation. What happens next?

Life becomes incredibly beautiful. We acquire an inner peace never known before, a balance and maturity in dealing with our problems and an enhanced skill in relating to others. The old neurotic rushing about and worrying about everything is over, we can roll with the punch. Because we have stopped burning off half our energies trying to think our way through everything and fretting about things which never happen, our mental and physical health improves and we look around to enjoy life in all its aspects, making new friends, taking on with new interests which are forever expanding. At last we know the secret of living and once the doing is being done, consistently and daily, there is 'nothing to it.'

We are right. But only half right. Marching along beside us every step of the way and never sleeping are the inherent pride, egotism and sloth of our human nature. Pride begins to tell us we've got it made. We've done the hard work, now it's time to sit back and enjoy the fruits. Egotism always has its own ideas and now that we've sorted ourselves out, it wants to get on with them. Sloth likes to forget and take things easy and it doesn't much like living on the hard edge of reality all the time. We slacken up on our efforts, slip into reverse gear and within a comparatively short time our negative emotions have taken us over and we're back again as worried and depressed as ever we were. With a feeling that the bottom has fallen out of the world, we begin to suspect that this thing doesn't work. Do not be upset. We all go through these passages. What is happening is not that it doesn't work but that it is we that don't work: we have neglected to do the doing. Life has to be lived every day. There is no time off for good behaviour and no public holidays. There never comes a point in anybody's life when they have got it made. Our pride, egotism and sloth go with us to the grave, and there is no known spiritual, psychological or physical surgery whereby they can be removed. Happiness doesn't float on the breeze. It has to be worked for; every day and all the days.

Now, pause for thought here. We can overdo the hard line bit when we warn each other that our new life takes doing. It does take doing and a lot of doing, but there is no need to make it sound more difficult than it is. Because something is difficult it does not mean that it is not exciting and enjoyable—as those certifiable people who beat hell out of innocent little white golfballs will be the first to tell you. If we carry the hardline attitude too far, we can give the impression that this is a joyless white knuckled business and that we are heroic martyrs. It's bad enough to give that impression to others but it's fatal to give it to ourselves. Life is to be enjoyed and not endured. If we are not doing a lot of laughing, there is something wrong and we need to sit down and have a long chat with our guide.

There is an other mistake we all make and maybe a word here will save you some embarrassment. A spiritual experience can be a heady affair. Our first impulse is to run to the roof top and shout it to the world. People who do that are usually taken down by the fire brigade while the world continues on its merry way, and we all know pain-in-the-neck people who spring to their feet and exclaim 'Praise the Lord' every time their cigarette lighter works. You and I may have the sense not to go that route, but yet another mistake may trip us up. As we grow in ourselves we begin to understand something of what makes people tick, and we begin to look around and take a healthy interest in other people and how they do their thing. We begin to notice that many of the people we looked up to and many others we thought of as 'normal'—whatever that may be—are not as together as we imagined. What we are seeing, of course, is nothing more than evidence of our common humanity. But we forget that. We get the crazy idea that we know the answer to the human problem. Not alone do we know it but we have some obligation to tell other people what it is. Understandably, this causes resentment and embarrassment. Other people, like ourselves, get by quite well by gift of God and a little help from their friends and have been doing it long before we came down off the mountain to save the world; so our best policy is to keep our mouths shut and our theories to ourselves and, as far as these things are concerned, to speak when we are spoken to and not before. If we find ourselves playing the 'helper' game—sniffing around for someone who needs to touch the hem of our garment and turning every conversation into a game of 'Let's play psychiatrist', we are not seeing others as equals but have wholly lost sight of our own vulnerability and humanity. There is a one hundred and eighty degree turn between being available and telling the world how to do it. Live and let live is the word.

Sometimes life *seems* to go very wrong indeed. We are flowing along nicely, all the days are good ones and the miracles are happening. Business goes well, we get a good job, the problems get mopped up and we are comfortable at last. The losing years are all behind us and from here on in we're going to win every round and show the crowd what we know. Then we get hit with a gut-shot which winds us. When we drop our elbow to guard the midriff, we get busted on the jaw; and when we try to fight back, we run into a combination we never saw coming and get slung through the ropes. If this is God's idea of being a friend, who needs an enemy? We are confused and disillusioned. Will some kind person tell us what is going on?

What's going on is that life isn't fair. It never was and it never will be. The non-smoking, non-drinking jogger drops dead at thirty. The hard-going hell raiser who smokes like a blast furnace and drinks diesel out of an old boot dies peacefully in his bed at a hundred and four surrounded by a loving family, fortified by the rites of Holy Mother Church. The frugal man lives in poverty while the last of the big spenders wins the lottery. We know all that and we accept it, but do we accept it for ourselves? Other people can lose their job, run out of readies and hit the wall but not us. We are special. We have chosen to run on an inside track and once we are fervent in our prayers God, God bless him, will do our divine will. Now we are utterly broken and confused. What are we to do? We hang in. We've signed on for the voyage and only a quitter jumps ship at Marseilles. If we do stay on board and ride out the storm, we come through our turmoil to a new understanding of reality. We see that we have been trading with God. We have held on to a personal agenda and tried to psyche God into seeing it through. We haven't really broken our pride and self-will. And so we reach what the high players call the second surrender. We see that accepting these ideas as very interesting theories is not the same thing as making them a way of life. Slowly we learn acceptance—but at deeper level. We see at last that what counts is not whether we are winning or losing but how we play each game. We come to see that any dilettante can look good with a following wind, but it takes a pro to keep getting up with a grin when one eye is closed. This time around we'll do it differently. This time we'll let God call the shots and take the pressure and we'll slip stream and do no more than our best. We'll do a little more consulting with our friends and guides, be a bit more honest in self-disclosure. Admit readily when we can't handle it, be quicker to seek help. In other words, we hand the hassle over and start living a day at a time and doing what we were created to do—enjoy life. We now see that the bad passage was not a setback but an essentially important experience which has given us a greatly developed capacity for peace and happiness, and as our humility has become genuine we need never be afraid again of going through tough times. At last we are freed of our selfish 'wants' and the haunting sense of insecurity. From now on our security is invested in some higher power and not in our personal ability to organise our own affairs. We begin to understand things in a new way. We see that things do not go well or go badly: they just go. What we really meant by things going well was that our ego, plans and convenience were being flattered. When we said that things were going badly we really meant that our self will and ambitions were being thwarted. We now know contentment, seeing that winning and losing are perceptions of the ego. They are not reality. And we come through with a heightened awareness of what reality is and a greater compassion for others who go through their own difficulties. This time out we'll do our best and no more. We'll play a long game. We'll sit and wait, flow with the river. We'll let things happen. And they do. In slow and mysterious ways we are guided along to the things we need for our own happiness. The shopping list is torn up and we know contentment. And the next time things go 'wrong' we are unconcerned for at last we know that we are being brought along to a better situation. Learning to trust doesn't come easy. There's a gap, wide as a wingspan, between saying it and doing it. We can throw ourselves to our knees and cry out 'Oh my Father, I trust in thee' (where *do* they get that crazy language—who would speak to a real father like that?)—and that's saying it. Can we sit in a fast car with an invisible driver who's hot and not blink when there's a tight corner coming up?—That's doing it.

Don't worry about it. We all think at the beginning we can't make it. The answer is we can and we do. The secret is we take care not to do it ourselves.

think page

Forget guilt. Sling it overboard. It doesn't help. At best it is the heart cry of self-injured innocence; at worst the strident shriek of pride in distress. Most of it was programmed into us when we were young to make us conform to the convenience of others.

We can be so sorry for what we've done that we'll do nothing to put it right. Forgive your own sins. God can't because He has never condemned you. Do something. Put it right. Straighten the record. Do better next time.

7 Altered attitudes

Most of us have fixed attitudes which colour our response to everything and which we have never thought out. Attitudes are no more than habits of thinking—the way we look at things. Attitudes can be very helpful. If our attitudes serve us well we live life almost on instinct without having to think out every situation we run into. It's good to be able to live on the automatic pilot without holding a public enquiry in our head every time we want to do something. But attitudes can be also very unhelpful and quite self destructive. The question is not, does our attitude agree with other peoples? but, Do our attitudes help us to live our life as a meaningful and happy experience? In other words, what kind of a script are we running in our minds which dictates our reactions to the realities around us. Are our attitudes helpful or unhelpful?

We don't have to think very hard to answer that one. If we have been suffering from constant worry and anxiety, recurrent depressions, it is obvious that we are responding to an inner script which is most unhelpful. Our emotional equipment, the way we habitually think and react, has not been working well. So we change it. Here we go again, more work.

Like everything else we have discussed we can either break the problem into simple parts or bend our brains with masses of irrelevant theory. But putting it simply, we rarely establish our own attitudes. Most of them are programmed into us by our parents and teachers and church leaders. If we are to deal with unhealthy attitudes we need to a) find out what they are, b) question their sources, and c) work to change them.

As before we must look to the three dimensions of reality we found out about:

GOD: What is our attitude to God? Do we believe in a sin-counting, punitive deity, who needs a continuous diet of human misery to keep him happy? Or do we know a loving Father who can only act in love? Which is it?

OURSELVES: Are we miserable sinners, rejected in the sight of God, born to suffer, who don't really deserve to get well and be happy? Or are we the specially marked out, unique and chosen children of an Almighty Father? Which is it?

OTHER PEOPLE: Do we see others as better, faster, smarter than ourselves, people we must either con or conquer to win the battle of life, or do we see them as brothers and sisters who share a common humanity with all its aches and pains, up days and down days, most of whom are really fine people when you get to know them? Which is it?

We must not skate over these questions. These attitudes are either healthy or unhealthy and we need to be fully aware which ones are ours.

LIFE: Life is a battle to be won, a problem to be solved. Nice guys come last and if we don't hang in there and hack it, we'll lose. Or life is an incredible mystery and there are no answers and it's a fun thing to kick it along from day to day watching how the world rolls on. Which is it? Or we have been very 'good' people and life 'owes' us something more than others.

It's quite obvious which is, not the 'right' answer, but which is the one with which we can be most comfortable. One set of answers places us under a lot of stress and the other makes for happy living. Which way do we intend to live?

Without drifting into weighty psychology, most of our unhealthy and deep seated attitudes we picked up came from childhood influences. If our parents, teachers and church leaders were infinitely wise, we would be very foolish to question what they taught us. But they weren't infinitely wise. Exactly as we are, they too were fallible humans, prey to their own pressures and hang-ups, quite capable of being as neurotic as we are and about some things, very wrong indeed. That does not make them bad people. It makes them human people. So in examining our attitudes we must learn to question our childhood influences and separate in a sensible way what is helpful to us from what is not. We have an obligation to live our own lives and formulate our own beliefs and values. We mustn't cop out by swallowing whole somebody else's game-plan and trying to piggy-back our lives on somebody else's answers. Our parents and teachers grew up in very repressive times. The innate dignity of the human person, the critical need for children to be affirmed and not undermined were not as clearly understood as they are now. There was a morbid theology that life was a vale of tears presided over by a punishing and angry God, and that children should be repressed into conformity. If we have done any work at all we have come to know a different God and developed some understanding of our own dignity, and we must challenge any attitude which conflicts with that experience.

We don't change inbuilt attitudes simply by taking a decision. We must first become conscious that we have an unhealthy attitude, watch for it and see how it drives us, and knock it on the head every time it comes up for air. That isn't easy to do. If we have been guilt-ridden or programmed with fear and remorse we must work hard to reverse this inner thinking. Here again we see the need to keep close contact with the person we have chosen to give us guidance. We cannot effect radical changes of thinking on our own: maybe that's the first attitude that needs changing.

In the context of coming to terms with childhood influences there is one particular worm which gnaws within and robs our peace of mind as nothing else can and that is resentment. In our examination of our attitudes most of us need to do a lot of work in this area. What exactly are we talking about?

The word 'resentment' means to 'feel again'. A resentment is a home movie we keep in our head which we run and run again until we know by heart every line and scene of it. If the movie was of happy days in the sunlight, there are a million worse ways of using our memory. But it isn't that kind of movie. The movie we label as a resentment is a scene of our being hurt, humiliated, embarrassed or unjustly treated by some person or situation in the past. The movie is expertly made. Every scene and word of it is diamond-bright, the soundtrack is quadro and we re-live again and again all the hurt and pain of the incident. The movie may be shot on location or in the studio (in other words our resentment may be real or imaginary), but it doesn't matter. It hurts us deeply, stirs us to fury and we vow vengeance, because if it takes us a million years we're going to settle scores and repay the wrong.

We can't reason ourselves out of a resentment. We know that resentment is a pointless exercise. The people we vow to catch up with are politely going about their own lives, wholly unaware that they are on our hit list and most certainly not thinking of us. And we, poor foolish mortals, have allowed them free lodgings in our head, permitting them to hurt us again and again—and we're paying the cameraman. We know perfectly well that there can be no peace of mind until we get rid of our collection of home movies. But how? Who wants such a collection? Let's face it, not easy to do.

For all the right reasons we can easily do the wrong thing. We can take a cold decision to 'leave all that behind' close down the cinema and pretend it never happened. But emotional pain must out. If we cement it down, it will smoulder away and burst out, and some psychiatrists claim that depression is an inward directed rage that has never been expressed where it should have been. We can also be hurt, decide at once to forget it and then find that, days later, some uneasy spectre is walking around in our head and we don't know what it is.

We need to go quickly to our chosen guide or good listener and report what happened. We don't slide over it. We report the incident—how we felt about it at the time and how we feel about it now. We express those feelings—the rage, the shame, the humiliation of it. The objectivity of the other person and our humility in revealing our pain and vulnerability defuses the incident of much of its power. We have taken action as opposed to sitting and trying to manage it on our own and that in itself will have its reward. We all find that many things which we thought would be very difficult to talk about seem quite trivial once we get them out.

We then brood a little on the person who hurt us, not in a vengeful way but in a compassionate and understanding way. There is no person under the sun in whom there is not some good, and if we think about the other fairly we will come to see that. We also apply a bit of fair play. There were times in the past when we ourselves were hurtful and unjust to others. Very sensibly we forgave ourselves. We acknowledged our human fallibility, accepted that there were times when we did very badly. Now we extend exactly the same tolerance to the other person. They may well have been very wrong to do or say what they did to us, but they have no monopoly of wrongdoing. It doesn't take a mathematician to work out that we should forgive them—unreservedly, and with the same open heart as we have forgiven ourselves.

And that's not enough. We can easily elevate ourselves on to a moral high by forgiving others. A moral high is a pedestal we should never get up on, for our heads can't stick the height. We take on a spurious nobility because we were so generous to forgive but we must push it past that: if we claim to be in touch with reality, we must see that there is nothing to forgive. Everybody, even the most disagreeable person, does the best he or she knows. If they knew better, they would do better. Given the limitations of the human condition, the circumstances of the situation and hidden pressures we knew nothing about, it was impossible for that person to behave in any other way at that time. Forget forgiving: there is nothing to forgive. Forgiving can be a very self-righteous pose indeed.

And if the people we are trying to absolve from our resentments happen to be parents or teachers, even that isn't enough—if we want to be real. We must bring ourselves to see that they did their best and it was a good best. It doesn't mean we must swallow everything which was laid on us in childhood—we owe it to ourselves to make our own rules and call our own shots—but it does mean that in our efforts to assert ourselves as human persons we must not discard the good with the bad or deny credit where it is due.

So, getting rid of resentments is not an event: it is a process, and it takes work. But if we are to be free in ourselves and know peace that work must be done. Resentments don't walk away; they just hide for a while and explode later at the worst possible moment. There is some evidence to suggest that many physical illnesses (such as heart conditions and cancers) may have their origins in suppressed resentments and harboured bitterness.

Consistently working through our old resentments in this way, and shedding the new ones as fast as we pick them up, does bring about a very basic change in our attitude to people around us. We shed our old prickly sensitivity and stop looking for occasions to be insulted. We stop the childish nonsense of demanding apologies and standing on some stupid dignity. An easy tolerance which we had to work to develop becomes reflex and we do develop a genuine indifference to the antics of others. On the other hand, if we do not go through this exercise we will be ruled forever from the past, ever ready to take offence, and our serenity can be whipped away by the first person we meet who is having a bad day.

There's an important other side to the coin of tolerance. Our inner peace must be precious to us. It is hard to get and at times hard to hold. We keep away from the people, places and things which unsettle us. It's a sad fact of life that some people never grow up, some are sicker than others, and there are those who run venom in their veins. They rejoice in gossip and the misfortune of others and are quite incapable of holding a conversation without airing their spite or setting up a confrontation. Some people can only stay afloat by pulling others down. There is no need for us to feel superior. These people have to function that way because they know no other. But nothing obliges us to hazard our serenity by contact with them. We tend to take in the emotional tone of those with whom we habitually associate. Stick with the happy people. Stay away from those who wallow in negative thinking. If we do have to meet them or tangle with them, we do our business quickly, tell them to have a nice day and run like hell.

We must work to make healthy attitudes a matter of automatic thinking. The soldier spends hours arms drilling and square bashing to condition himself respond unthinkingly to the word of command. It sounds very stupid. But his purpose is to condition himself to react automatically so that when he is under fire and rational thinking is difficult, he can save his life and those of his comrades by doing on reflex what an untrained person would have to think out—if he could. It is the very same for us in our attitudes. If we are to live as relaxed and easy people, we must work consciously so that our responses to the various situations of life become unthinking reflexes. Like the soldier, we need to be automatic in our certainty that God as we understand him loves and approves of us, that we love and approve of ourselves, and that all the people we meet are exactly like ourselves, good and worthy people doing the best they can in at times very difficult circumstances. The more we embed these attitudes into our repertoire of reflex thinking, the easier life is going to be.

If we truly trust a Creative Intelligence to provide for our needs and guide our lives, we can afford to stop fighting anything or anybody. We don't have to compete or outdistance our fellow man. We don't have to have answers to every problem or think everything out. Some of us have an obsession with knowing things and understanding everything. We can read all the books and just find out more things to be ignorant about. There is an awful lot going on which is the business of our Father and not of ours. How do we train ourselves into a new attitude? Attitudes, as we saw, are habitual patterns of thinking. By constantly thinking over our new attitudes, practising them, psyching ourselves, as the athletes call it, we bring the thought down from our minds into our reflexes just as the soldier on the drill square spends hour after hour after hour doing exactly the same thing.

think page

When I became a man I put away the things of a child. Don't demand apologies. Demands for apologies are schoolyard tactics, games we left behind when we grew up.

People wrong us because they know no better. They think they have to be that way. If we think we know better, let's act better.

Never forgive. Come to see that there is nothing to forgive.

8 Keeping it simple

Of all the people in the world, we are the ones who need to rubber-stamp the phrase 'Keep it simple' on the back of our hand. If we have a history of depressive illness, anxiety states or thought patterns of worry, we have built up a mental habit of intellectualising, trying to think everything out and know all the answers. Look back and see how it happened.

When we were young our teachers used to say, 'Think, think. Use your head.' They were right, of course. You cannot work out the cube root of pi unless you think about it. But we misused the message. We thought that if we amassed a stock of answers and used our brains, we could think our way through every problem which came along. For a while it worked. We could in fact reason out anything which came along—up to a point. Then life threw a few curves, the 'think, think, think' didn't work and every certainty we ever had crumbled in ashes. But we didn't learn. We thought even harder. Round and round we spun our brains, trying to figure the odds and work out the problem. And in the process we became very complicated people. We could not accept that there are many of life's problems which cannot be solved by thinking things out, and there are some which can't be solved at all. We did not accept that all reality is an interweave of the material and the spiritual which cannot be worked out in exclusively human terms. Now we have to reverse all that and learn to use our minds in a sensible way.

The message we share in these pages is one of the most beautiful simplicity. Simple does not necessarily mean easy, it means that it is not complicated. But there are apparent contradictions which, if we can endure yet an other contradiction, we need to think out; and to do this, we must, believe it or not, think about how we think.

The Pueblo Indians of New Mexico astounded Carl Jung with their belief that the white man is mad because he thinks in his head. I suppose it is not for nothing we refer to 'head cases' and tap our foreheads when we meet somebody madder than ourselves. The Indian thinks in his heart and the more primitive tribes think low in the stomach, and when we see the growing chaos of the western world we might well wonder if they haven't the right idea after all. But as we grow, we begin to develop some respect for the 'opposite sex' side of our minds. Men learn to start using the receptive, intuitive, feminine side. Women learn to use the logical, deductive, male side. We learn that much of our thinking can be safely entrusted to the never sleeping subconscious, and the gut instinct and the hunch when to play it and when to restrain it can be relied upon safely. We can face life with a new confidence that once we stop the furious forebrain thinking, working the head, the subconscious dreaming self, is free to carry its end of the plank and the human mind is a far more sophisticated and superb mechanism than we ever dared to believe. Now we can look at the apparent contradictions without being too dismayed or trying to reason it all out with intellectual argument.

Where lies the even balance between:

1. Doing the doing, and letting things happen?

2. Honest effort, and not trying too hard?

3. Being sincere, without taking things seriously?

4. Letting God run our lives, and calling our own shots?

5. Being ourselves, and keeping the ego in check?

There are no quick answers to these questions in a logical form but the answer lies in 'the wisdom to know the difference.' An exterior guidance system. Many people who live this life make constant use of the Serenity Prayer:

> God grant me the serenity
> to accept the things I cannot change,
> courage to change the things I can
> and the wisdom to know the difference.

And there lies our answer, the constant asking for wisdom to know the difference. Wisdom is not stored in the head where we keep the knowledge we constantly forget. It is not stored at all. It comes in the heart when it is needed and not before. Despite all that we will be mistaken at times and we can expect that; but, as we will see, the world will not fall down and we learn to make our decisions and live with the consequences. If we're wrong about something we can admit it at once and correct course.

How do we know when we're flying out of balance, falling short of the 'wisdom to know the difference?' Quite subtly the ego (Edging God out) can get its hands on the controls and we start flying out of trim and losing air speed. The stall warning (Fear) blows. Fear (Feck Everything And Run) tells us that we've distanced ourselves from the Father and got back to running our own show. This warning is not a disaster. It is there to assist us. And we get back to level flight by letting the pilot do the flying. In other words, the apparent contradictions need not trouble us as we have a built in stall warning to keep the balance between the extremes. 'Knowing' answers is not important.

We can also complicate our lives by trying to solve all our problems by the weekend, taking on inner pressures we don't need. As we saw, life moves on from one unresolved situation to another and the only constant is change. There will never come a day when we can put a tick against every problem we have, and as fast as we tick one off another has presented itself for attention. We had better accept that, for it may come as a surprise to us. We had always thought that if we tried hard enough we could cross a line and find everything in order. Not so. If we are of perfectionist turn of mind we must learn to accept disorder in small things so that there can be order in greater things.

We can demand too much of ourselves, lay expectations on ourselves which are unreasonable, deny or forget our humanity. This doesn't work either. We can try how we will, do all the doings but our humanity remains with us and we'll be far more at ease when we accept that and stop taking ourselves too seriously. It's OK to be depressed, bored, lonely and angry at times. It's OK to fall short, clip the rim and miss dead centre. It's OK not to know and have to ask somebody and it's OK to have to report in and confess we've done it badly and need to talk things out. If we've any sense of humour at all and we're looking for amusement, let us look to ourselves. We are, arguably, the best comedians we know.

Life is not allotted to us in leasehold tenures of months or years but in daily instalments of twenty-four hours, if not heartbeat by heartbeat. We see that every day. If we are anything over twenty-five, we have already seen some school friends with nothing wrong with them go down and not get up. Nothing makes us different. The Creator designed our minds to handle living a day at a time: 'Take no thought for tomorrow' said Jesus, who knew something of the God bit. But this is too simple for us. We want to stitch down tomorrow and nail down the agenda for next week. The stall warning (Fear and worry) blows because we are flying it out of trim, using our minds outside the manufacturer's specifications. The imagination was given to us to enable us visualise our goals, presuppose progress, anticipate joy. But we, thinking we must live alone, have trained ourselves to misuse this wonderful panorama as a theatre of the terrible to terrorise ourselves with vistas of potential disaster. We might say as much about memory. Memory is the wonderful data disc by which we can access lessons learned and happy days gone by. But we, thinking that life is a vale of tears, misuse it to re-run battles long ago and old sadnesses we should have worked through. Of course, misery is optional. If some tape is running in my head which I don't like, it's up to me to change it. And I can if I want to. The only reality is 'now'. And every time we slip into the future wrongly (misuse of imagination) or lapse into a bad past (misuse of memory), we are diminishing our contact with the now (reality.) Far better to keep the dreams until we fall asleep.

So we keep it simple. A mystery is a mystery because it's supposed to be a mystery and we accept that. We learn to train ourselves away from our obsessional wanting to know everything and confine ourselves to what we need to know. We need to know very little. There are many great wonders going on all round us and when we train ourselves to look with our inner eyes and listen with our hearts we can come upon enough magic in a days journey to amaze the Wizard of Oz. Life itself, our own selves, the next person, are utterly fascinating; and wonder is endless. We will never meet anybody who doesn't have a story to tell or who can't teach us something. And life goes on, becoming incredibly interesting and exciting, and, wearing the world like a loose garment, we go with it.

think page

Don't do other people's thinking for them. If you want to know what I think, ask me. Don't tell me, because you don't know until I tell you.

We are not responsible for what other people think. We are only responsible for what we do. What other people think is no concern of ours; that's their problem. What will the neighbours think? Nothing. They are not thinking of us at all. They are much too busy thinking about themselves. When did you last think of what the neighbours were doing?

Learn to say 'No'. If we approve of ourselves, we needn't worry who doesn't. We either live our lives as our own people or as crowd pleasing 'yes men', ever up on our hind legs, wagging our tails and begging for a pat on the head. Say 'No' sometimes. We were not put into the world to live up to other people's expectations or suit their selfish convenience.

I am not responsible for the thoughts which come into my head. I am only responsible for what I do about them.

9 What is this thing called love?

Selfishness has no moral value, there's no 'wrong' or 'right' about it. It's a symptom of pain. If you doubt that startling proposition, try a simple experiment. Get yourself a presentable hammer and treat yourself to a whack on the thumb. Now, give an honest answer to a straight question: Are you thinking of yourself or other people?

We are not playing games here or telling funny jokes: we are facing up to something in ourselves which must be faced. Depression, anxiety, fear and worrying are very painful but self-absorbing disorders. We have been very selfish, you and I, and we may have made it a way of life without knowing what we were doing. Not a pleasant admission to have to make, but as that's the story we better deal with it. Nothing is served by hanging our heads and beating our breasts. Furthermore, we didn't opt to become depressed, inward looking, and selfish. On the contrary, by doing the work we have been doing we have eased a lot of the pain out, and as time goes by we're going to feel better and better and become quite fun people to live with. But the record is there and we must examine our concept of love and answer the songwriter's question: What is this thing called love?

We can answer the man in his own lyrics and say that love is the tender trap and the magnificent obsession and miss the point and intellectualise it and get nowhere. Keeping it simple, to love somebody, spouse, lover, child, parent or friend is a decision to work for their happiness and want nothing back. There must be better definitions, but ours is close enough to the best to work with.

Love is a free, no return transaction. Once we take the stance 'I'll love you if you love me', it's a trade-off. We trade with people every day—but we don't call it love. Love is a decision, an act of the will and—Sammy Kahn and Jimmy Van Heusen eat your hearts out—it isn't something we fall into. What is true is that in romantic love there is a large element of violins in-the-moonlight and trips to the moon on gossamer wings (who would want it otherwise?), but the bottom-line commitment is the free, no-return transaction. Obviously we take care about making such a commitment. We don't pledge it to somebody who'll scare the bejasus out of us when we wake up beside them in the morning. So, here we want to review the things we have learned about the human condition, understand our definition of love and apply the principles in the home. If we are street angels and house devils, we are not yet 'together', for being 'together' means that we drop the roles and integrate the diverse sides of our personality into one real person. If we have a beaming smile for the neighbours and a scowl for those at home, we have some getting together to do.

We already know that every human person has a unique and awesome personal dignity which is given by God and that there are no circumstances in which it can be lost or taken away. For some reason we can learn to concede this to outsiders but in our own homes we often behave as if different rules applied to our spouses and children. This is not something we would express or be aware of consciously. It is more a subtlety which comes over in our conduct. Here's a little scenario to make us nostalgic:

In times of stricter tempo often referred to as 'the good old days', Papa waxed his moustache, wore a gold watchchain across his paunch and Papa's home was his castle and Papa's word was law. And all the people in Papa's castle (wife, child or the unfortunate girl who polished the brass knocker) were the obedient servants of Papa's every wish and whim. All the arrangements of the household were scheduled to Papa's comings and goings and if Papa was reading the paper, having a sulk or above in the bed convalescing from a feed of drink, everybody tiptoed about in quaking dread until Papa rose from the dead and gave permission for normal breathing to be resumed. Papa dictated the religious, political and social opinions of the household and nobody ever thought to question them. 'Ah, lawksey me, them were the days. There was no sex or television them times, I'll tell you, and we got on just as well.'

The song is ended but the melody lingers on. If we take away Papa's watchchain, shave off his moustache, and substitute for the brass knocker one of those godawful door chimes, we may see in our touching evocation of Papa a disturbing outline of ourselves. It may even happen that Papa is alive and well and living in our homes. It follows that if Papa is to be given the decent burial to which he is entitled after all these years we must question some of our attitudes and measure them up against our professed respect for the dignity of the other people in our homes. Forgive me here (and, indeed, elsewhere) for being unable to avoid sexist overtones without going into the husband/wife, him/her school of literature, but whether we are men or women the questions posed and the ideas we are discussing have some application to all of us.

1. Is my wife free to come and go as she pleases without consulting me or accounting for where she has been?

2. Is my spouse free to hold religious, political, and social opinions different from mine, express them freely in public and argue with me in support of them?

3. In joint decisions, which of us has the final word and why?

4. If somebody asks me what my wife thinks about a topic or controversy, do I answer them or tell them to go and ask her?

5. Is it 'my' money or 'our' money? If it's 'our' money, why isn't it in a joint account? Or maybe I like to control others by obliging them to ask for what is theirs?

There are no right answers to these questions (and in a caring relationship where spouses are also friends and lovers they rarely arise), but they pose in turn another question which summarises all the questions which do arise:

If I insist on my own individual dignity and personal freedom, am I prepared to promote and vindicate the same dignity and freedom in someone I'm supposed to love—even to the point where some of their chosen values will differ from mine and they're hell bent on doing something I don't want but they have a right to do?

As we saw earlier, answers are not too important but the questions test the reality of the progress we have been trying to make.

Here's another we raised before: Can I accept, and how deeply do I accept, that a spouse is always human and at times will be tired, bloodyminded, wrong, and not only have off-moments but off-days and -weeks. We can't have it both ways. We can either marry a human being or pray heaven to send down an angel or a saint; or else we can go for the pale insipid type who'll tell you're right every time, agree with everything you do and walk ten paces behind. And when the relationship withers away from shrieking boredom, it's tough all round but you could have had a far livelier time if you had bagged one of the real flesh-and-blood ones who'd love you tenderly today and tell you go to hell tomorrow for at least you'd have had to work at it and, whatever befalls, your marriage would never grow stale.

Work at it?   Life moves on, we change and grow older. There can't ever come a time in a relationship when no further effort is needed for any relationship is either getting better or worse. No matter how good it is,if we do nothing it will get worse. There is no holding pattern where we can circle around admiring the view. These are the vibrant bustling years; there's a schoolbag on every step of the stairs and a roller skate under your bum every time you sit down. But, fast enough to make you blink, the house will empty and the last of the girls will fly out to Danbury, Conn. to marry some young fellow with a squeaky voice who does something with recirculating ball bearings and for the first time in over a quarter of a century you'll be left alone with either a mean-minded sparring partner who'll throw a dirty punch every time (and wherever did she learn those back alley tricks?) or a spouse, lover, confidant, and best friend.

Marriage, no matter what the celibates say (isn't it extraordinary what these chaps know about love, sex, and marriage?) is not for ever, it's only for today. We just have to work at it for today. Just for today you must target somebody, study their needs, feel their pain, listen out for what is not being said and often enough do no more than be there. Love costs. It plays havoc with personal convenience, patience, tolerance and the selfish self; but it takes a pro, and if we can't go the distance we shouldn't have got into the ring. But one day, if we've always demanded the best of ourselves and given something more, we'll look back on all the up-days and down-days, all the winning and losing, birthdays and birthdays forgotten and all those moments when we let the side down by thinking of something else, and know that there isn't one other person on the planet we'd have gone the years with and we'd never have wanted it any other way. And autumn in the park need not be sad.

Meanwhile, who makes our rules?

- Do the Jones decide what we will wear, drive, buy, and what clubs or associations we are 'expected' to join?

- Are we living to the reality of our income or busting a financial gut to put in double-glazing because 'everyone' around here has it?

- Do we decide between us what our sexual ethics and practices shall be or do we listen to vegetarians when we want to fry steak?

- Do we decide whether we want to go to hear some Chinese poetry reading or is that something decided for us by Mummy, The Parish Committee, Auntie Nell, or Mrs Cockfosters Mainbearing?

And what about those birds of passage life dropped into our nest for safekeeping which we mistakenly call 'our' children? Just because another human being is smaller, more impressionable, more vulnerable and dependent, by what argument is the dignity of that person less than mine? Have 'our' children been sent into the world—a matter upon which they were not consulted—to be themselves in their own way or to be secondhand carriers of our opinions, social aspirations and failed ambitions? Are we bringing them up or letting them grow up? Are we setting them free or tying them up? Do we affirm them again and again by praise and encouragement, applaud their initiatives and draw them out or do we squash them down, repress them into submission and blow a gasket if there's white flour or black paint around first time they try to bake a cake or paint a gate? Are we cramping them with constant correction, rules and regulations all designed to suit our comfort and convenience, making them whipping posts for our fatigues and bad humour? Can we run sensible risks and live with a reasonable anxiety level as we gradually set them free to go out into the world in prudent stages? Can we be open with them, labelling our opinions as opinions, inviting their comments and possible disagreement or do we subject them to mealtime monologues in which we air our prejudices to a captive audience. Can we go the extra mile and concede to them that there are some subjects upon which we do have prejudices which we have yet to work out of our system? Can we accept that children are naturally noisy and high-spirited and if they weren't there would be something very wrong? Are we running a military outpost, a contemplative monastery or a loving home?

There are ways of saying 'No', drawing the line, encouraging the consideration to which others are entitled without employing Papa's searing sarcasm or the ever constant threat of a 'clip in the ear.' Can we be real enough to jettison the old 'head of the household' nonsense and live in a democracy of loving, give and take affability and yet be political enough to rig the election if the five year old wants his 'go' at the power drill? In sum, can we hit that fine balance between the liberty of the person and the license of the ego?

Here's a subtle one: If we stop teaching our children for a while we may learn something from them. Have we ever seen anyone live KEEP IT SIMPLE and A DAY AT A TIME better? What comment did Jesus make in his own time about becoming as little children? If you want free, in-house lessons in living watch your children, and the smallest ones most of all.

What is this thing called love? There must be a million answers but whatever it is, it starts at home.

think page

There is no such thing as a bad day. There is such a thing as a difficult day. That's up to me. I can decide whether it's going to be difficult or fun.

Split your worries into two piles. The ones you can do something about—do it. The ones you can do nothing about—forget it. But what will happen? We don't know. We don't run the show. Those who think they do are playing God. A hard act to follow.

10 Reprise—Play it again, Sam

It's the witching hour when the warlocks walk and the night wind flings rain against the window. Time to wrap this thing up and go home, but before we do, let's play a few rideout riffs and look around to make sure we haven't left anything behind.

The bad news is that it takes time; progress is slow; it takes daily doing for a lifetime; we never have it made and easy, it is not. There is no other bad news. If we can buy that, we are unstoppable. There is no catch, no small print we haven't accepted. If these conditions did not apply we'd both end up with something neither of us would want to have. We both know from sad experience that the soft options don't work and the plastic stuff can't stand the heat.

The good news is that there isn't a book ever written which can describe it, for there are certain things like how high is up, what colour is the wind and human happiness which nobody has ever succeeded in putting into words which could tell the story. But there are some things we can say. It gets easier, miracles happen, things get better, the only requirement is a willingness to keep trying and we never have to go it alone. It is nowhere written that we must do it right. If it were, those of us who try to live this way would have sunk without trace years ago. The only demand is that we take action and do our best. Nothing says that we have to understand how it works, be concerned and anxious, and sit staring into our navel wondering how we are getting on. Deserving, being worthy of, meriting has nothing to do with it. Putting it in a nutshell, if we do the doing it will work in spite of us. There is nothing mysterious about that. If you visit an airfield, you will see exactly the same thing.

A plane takes off and flies because the pilot guns up the engine, lets it roll along the runway and then tilts the wings into a certain angle of attack. At takeoff speed the aircraft becomes airborne. It becomes airborne because the pilot has taken certain actions and the aircraft answers to the inflexible laws of aerodynamics. And it doesn't matter whether the pilot thinks about it, has faith, understands the principles, is relaxed about it or very worried. In fact, given the action taken, the plane will lift in spite of the pilot. No other result is possible. The doing has been done and up she goes. And the plane doesn't care whether the pilot is a nice guy or beats his wife. Our situation is identical. There are certain inflexible laws of growth and happiness and when we take certain actions these laws apply. We do what we must and we grow into happiness. No other result is possible.

We are, each and all of us, very important people. That wasn't a claim we thought up to make us feel good; it is something God ordained. And we need to be very clear why. We cannot build a healthy self image on shifting sands. Our dignity and importance rests upon our being children of God. Unless we work to internalise that value, it's a central reality we haven't accepted and it's nothing more than another piece of religious rhetoric. So we do need to think about it, contemplate it constantly and make up our mind whether it's going to be just one more pious phrase we use or something we know. An attitude. If, on the other hand, we haven't taken this in deep and we rest our self esteem on a position in life, our supposed achievements, our ability to acquire coin of the realm (or indeed the absence of these things), we're building on very quirky ground. Circumstances may change and often do—riding high today, shot down in May—and if our self worth is based on anything external to us we are going to be very broken people if it is threatened or taken away. But if our value is located within, nothing can lay a glove on us. We're less open to flattery and manipulation and we can't be bought. We're out of the rat race and increasingly indifferent to winning or losing. If, on the other hand, our ego has stitched us into tinsel things, we pay an awesome price. We're scrambling up the peak in Darien, busting a gut to get there and ever afraid of being passed out or losing our footing. We survive by fighting the world, hustling to outmanoeuvre everybody else, and we'll always have to sleep with one eye open watching the bottom line. If we kick and scratch hard enough, we may well get up there, and many people do; but it isn't a good way to be comfortable, because sooner or later we must meet somebody who can kick and scratch harder. Does that mean that we turn our faces from success and human achievement, in so far as there is such a thing? It means that we do our best, stop worrying and allow God to slot us in life where he best wants to have us—an infinitely wise decision he takes in our best interests. At the same time it's a great mistake to think that people who have done well in life have got there unfairly. It's a greater mistake to think that people who live in quiet obscurity are not highly successful top flight people. We'll meet top people in the palaces of the great and the places of the poor. And we'll meet very sad and disturbed people in both and midway between.

Settling our self-esteem on an inner value involves tearing up the conventional thinking of the world—calling our own shots. Much of the advertising business functions on the psychology of human avarice, insecurity and immaturity. Drive this, drink that, dwell there, and you're somebody. The financial institutions do much business on the same basis. Sign here and we help you acquire the assets to be somebody. Every time we open a paper or watch television we are being washed over subtly, subliminally, constantly and blandly with the same message, and it takes a lot of growing up to recognise the lie and kick the system. But that's what we have been saying. Either we determine our values or the advertising people will do it for us and if we allow that we'll end up being very uncomfortable and never know why.

We can also run out the other end of the same tunnel and feel guilty and unworthy about having a few toys to play with and enjoying the game. If we can afford to do it, let's be people of simple tastes—nothing but the best! It really doesn't matter whether we have a Ferrari in the stable or not; the hard question is, Are we driving the car or is the car driving us? What is essential is that we recognise what matters and what doesn't.

Most of all serenity means handling the niggling pinpricks of life. For some reason most of us rise well to major stress and if the house catches fire we'll be the only one to keep our head. It's when we break a shoelace we're really thrown. The answer is that we make the Serenity prayer our own and ponder as a habit its many hidden meanings. It's a personal opinion and no more that anybody who knows the Lord's Prayer and the Serenity Prayer knows them all; but, then again, that's the kind of personal opinion which gets people burnt at the stake. Don't tell anyone I said that.

As we go on we learn to slow down, sit and wait, postpone our satisfactions and let things come about. Fritz Perls said it well: 'Don't push the river; it flows by itself.' There is a pace, there is a time. We cannot work this out at intellectual level. If we try to, we can come up with many good and sufficient reasons for doing ten contradictory things at the same time. Let it happen. Let's keep out of our own light.

And we don't talk any more about nerves, worry and depression, because that's living in the problem. We talk about peace and happiness and the 'how to' of it all. That's living in the solution.

What's it all about? Mostly it's about enjoying life, being good to ourselves, being glad to be alive; exulting in simple things, comfortable in your own company, glad you lived to see today—any day. It's about waking up with a buzz of excitement, knowing always that the best is yet to be, nostalgia for the future. It's about shovelling it around when you can and finding you've got even more of it than when you started out. It's about writing and reading this book together for the rest of our lives and wincing wryly when your own words jump off the page and bite you. It's about knowing that you can't walk it as well as you talk it and even that doesn't matter as long as you're trying to.

Peace of mind? There isn't a description that I could write, and maybe only a poet should try; but there is a test we can apply. Can we live each moment of our lives so that if the old guy with the scythe taps us on the shoulder and says 'We're leaving in five seconds', we can turn, look him in the eye and say without a quaver, 'OK, old man, let's go!' If I could get it together, wrap it up in a ball and kick it to you, that's what I'd most want to give you.